Knowing
GOD'S WILL
For Your Life

By
Morris Cerullo

3rd Printing 2004
2nd Printing 2000
1st Printing 1990

**For a free book and tape catalog
of all Morris Cerullo messages,
write to:**

Morris Cerullo World Evangelism
P.O. Box 85277
San Diego, California 92186-5277

Morris Cerullo World Evangelism of Canada
P.O. Box 3600,
Concord, Ontario L4K 1B6

Morris Cerullo World Evangelism
P.O. Box 277
Hemel, Hempstead, HERTS HP2 7DH

"Now therefore, I pray thee, if I have found grace in thy sight, shew me now thy way, that I may know thee..." (Exodus 33:13).

"...be transformed (changed) by the (entire) renewal of your mind—by its new ideals and its new attitude—so that you may prove (for yourselves) what is the good and acceptable and perfect will of God, even the thing which is good and acceptable and perfect (in His sight for you)" (Romans 12:2, TAB).

TABLE OF CONTENTS

Dedication

With all my heart, I lovingly dedicate this book to Theresa, my faithful wife of over 50 years, who has stood by my side and has supported the call of God on my life to take the revelation of God and the power of His resurrected Son to the nations of the world.

As a faithful mother, Theresa has, by her endearments, earned the loving respect of our three children: David, Susan and Mark.

As a young man of 17, I was invited to be the special speaker at a chapel service of the Assemblies of God Bible Institute in Suffern, New York, where I met Theresa for the first time.

After the chapel service, Theresa and I were assigned to sit next to each other at the luncheon table. After lunch, I asked her to join me in the hallway. I pointed my finger at her and said, "Before I leave today, I just wanted to tell you one thing. Someday I'm coming back and I'm going to marry you."

Two years later, Theresa became my wife. This is evidence of how God's will can be revealed and manifested.

Theresa is affectionately called "Mama" by literally millions of people from around the world. Because of her sacrifices and compassionate love for the nations, I dedicate this book to this great woman of God...wife...mother...and real champion of the Lord.

Introduction

Every year an amazing species of bird called the lesser white-throated warbler hatches its young in Germany. Toward the end of each summer, the parents of these hatchlings fly off to spend the winter near the headwaters of the Nile River in Africa, leaving their babies behind.

However, before the cold sets in, these young birds also leave Germany, making their way to Africa by themselves without any prior knowledge, training, or example. Yet, in God's perfect timing, they land in the precise spot on the Nile where their parents are headquartered!

How do they do it? Scientists have discovered that these wonderful creatures actually have an inherited, inborn "navigational system" which even allows them to tell direction, latitude and longitude by the stars. They are created with all the knowledge they need to get where God intends for them to go.

But, as amazing as these birds are, they are not unique.

Over and over again, we see how God's creations—from the tiniest organisms to the tallest trees—grow to maturity and live in perfect harmony with His laws and His plan for their lives.

Yet, in stark contrast to all these wonders of nature are the tragic, desperate letters I receive from human beings—my dearest partners whom I love so much, but who are in a desperate struggle to find God's will for them!

You cannot imagine what agony Theresa and I experience when we hear partners with their bodies ravaged by cancer ask us if this suffering is God's will!

Every week we hear parents with drug-addicted or suicidal children cry out, "Brother Cerullo, we go to church every week and love the Lord. How did we get out of His will?"

Other believers are trapped in financial poverty, battered marriages, broken homes and dead-end jobs. All of them are asking the same thing: "Could this possibly be God's will for my life?"

Then there are the countless Christians who are not currently undergoing any personal crises, but who fervently desire to do more for the Lord in this last harvest time cycle. Daily, they petition Him for clearer direction and more definite guidance.

But no matter what the situation, the vast majority of the letters I receive have one common thread, and that is, "Brother Cerullo, how can I learn to hear God for myself, so I can know His will every day of my life?"

Beloved, this is a question that has haunted me day after day, as the mail continues to pour in.

How, I wondered, could birds and all of nature live in such perfect harmony with God's will, maturing into exactly what they were created to be, when His **own children,** the born-again sons of God, agonize over the question of whether debilitating diseases, sin, and degrading defeat by the enemy are His will for their lives!

How is it that a caterpillar is effortlessly transformed into a magnificent butterfly, while the very sons of the Creator are confused as to Who He is, and who they are to become in Him?

God has ordained that His sons in Christ are to be the highest form of creation next to the God-head itself! So why is it that we, who have the "Navigational System" of the universe dwelling within us, do not know which way to turn?

How can each of us learn to be "in touch" with the voice of God within our hearts, so that we can come to live in a rhythm of continually knowing (and being in harmony with) His perfect will?

My search for the answers to these questions brought me to other ones which are closely related—questions such as:

"Is God in absolute control of every detail of our lives?"

"Are a man's outward circumstances an indication of whether he is in or out of the will of God?"

"Is it possible to truly come to know God's will as it applies to the personal, intimate aspects of our individual situations?"

"What is God's ultimate purpose for our lives?"

As I pondered all of these things, a song my staff sings in chapel ran through my mind. It says:

"For I was born to be thy dwelling place

A home for the Presence of the Lord.

So let my life now be separated unto Thee,

That I might be what I was born to be."

Believe me, I know how deeply each one of you yearns to be united to Him in that powerful, life-giving relationship that He created you to have.

There isn't one of you whose heart doesn't cry out to know—and be completely fulfilled in—His perfect will. And this is what God longs for, too!

You cannot imagine how He longs for you to learn first how to hear and discern His voice, and then to apply what you hear so that you may come into a new rhythm of His victory, love and power!

I know that deep within, you have never been more hungry for God to strip away the mask, the insulation, and all the things that would hinder you from laying hold of Him so that His Life can flow through you uninterrupted.

Well, you are about to enter into a "new spiritual dimension"—one in which God is going to do a major work of restoring you to Himself. He is going to bring you into the light of His love and revelation of Himself that you have only scratched the surface in understanding.

Let us now go on to discover how each one of us can enter into a new dimension of intimacy with Him, and harmony with His perfect will.

Chapter 1

What are we really seeking?

"...truly our fellowship is with the Father, and with his Son Jesus Christ" (I John 1:3).

The first thing we must ask ourselves as we pursue the subject of knowing God's will is, "Exactly what do we mean when we say we are seeking to know the perfect will of God?"

After all, God's Word is His will. From Genesis to Revelation, every passage of Scripture vibrates with our Father's instructions to us.

But in talking with many of my partners, I have discovered that what they really hunger for is to have a particular passage "leap off" the page and into their hearts, so that they know that they **know, that they know**, without a doubt that a specific passage is His personal Word to them that day.

What they all want to know is that through His Word we are in communion with Him concerning whatever challenges we are facing.

When we face a difficult situation or are on the crossroads of a crucial decision, each one of us wants to learn to hear

His voice deep in our hearts saying, "Child, this is the way, walk ye in it."

Therefore, what is it that each of us is truly seeking?

It is a revelation of God Himself...the experience of the Master's "still, small voice" deep in our hearts. How we thirst for firsthand communication with Him...yet, we don't know how to go about finding it.

At times He will communicate His will to us by sending someone with a word of wisdom, a word of knowledge or prophecy. But we are not to look for or rely on this experience. God arranges circumstances as a confirmation of His Word.

Occasionally, He will even honor "fleeces" which His children put out, as Gideon did in the book of Judges (Judges 6:36-39).

Although these ways of receiving direction from God are valuable, they still do not fill the deep, inner emptiness that each of us has within our hearts for true fellowship and communion with our Lord and our Father that brings the will of God into our lives as a direct result.

Thus, I began to ask myself, "What is the **key** to coming into this kind of communion with God? A communion whereby living in His will means living in minute-to-minute fellowship with Him."

As I searched the Scriptures for an answer, I was soon led to a shocking revelation:

In verse after verse I found that we are commanded to act...to do the will of God, and to obey the will of God. But nowhere did I find any mention of how to know the will of God.

In every instance where the will of God is mentioned, it is associated with doing...not trying to figure it out.

In the book of Ephesians, Paul commands us: *"Therefore do not be vague and thoughtless and foolish, but understanding and firmly grasping what the will of the Lord is" (Ephesians 5:17, TAB).*

The Psalmist David rejoiced in the fact that, *"I delight to do thy will, O my God: yea, thy law is within my heart" (Psalm 40:8).*

And our Lord Himself boldly declared: *"...I came down from heaven, not to do mine own will, but the will of him that sent me...My meat is to do the will of him that sent me, and to finish his work" (John 6:38, 4:34).*

Gradually, as I continued to seek the Lord for keys to coming into deep, ongoing communion with Him, a new revelation began to unfold.

RESTORATION
God's ultimate will for your life
It's harvest time!

God spoke to me several years ago and revealed to me that we are entering into an endtime harvest cycle which would be marked by various manifestations.

Phase one: God is going to have a people.

Phase two: God's people must practice what they preach.

Phase three: God's people will enter a rhythm of miracle living.

Phase four: God is planting a new seed of revelation, love, faith and power in the lives of His people.

God works in cycles. A cycle is "an interval of time during which a sequence of a recurring succession of events or phenomena is completed."

All of these manifestations will continue throughout the cycle but when the harvest cycle is over, that's it! Jesus is coming.

This final harvest is more than a period of time in which to reap souls. It is actually a cycle in which God's people are being built up in their inner man to be reconciled to their full, intimate fellowship with Him!

As the Apostle Paul prophesied: *"May He grant you out of the rich treasury of His glory to be strengthened and reinforced with mighty power in the inner man by the (Holy)* Spirit *(Himself)*—indwelling your innermost being and personality"* (Ephesians 3:16, TAB).

Yes, this is a cycle in which the life of Christ Himself is being actively formed in the innermost lives of His saints *(Ephesians 3:17-20).*

Being a cycle, this harvest has stages of inner spiritual growth. In these stages, God is making us aware that He is going to have a people! They are going to be a people who will be endowed with a new inner strength to practice what they preach, what they read, and what they believe.

Then, empowered with His inner strength, these people will enter into a new rhythm of victory miracle living, proving to all the world that God's Son, Jesus, is alive.

It is during these stages of growth that God will do a major work of reconciling us to communication with Himself through His Son and His Spirit—a work which He has purposed since the fall of man in the Garden of Eden.

You see, when God created man, He created Him for the express purpose of fellowship with Himself, but He didn't want fellowship with robots. God wanted a people who would love Him because they wanted to love Him; who would serve Him because they wanted to serve Him; who would obey Him because they wanted to obey Him.

Therefore, He gave man a free moral will. It was up to man to decide if he would choose to love God.

Unfortunately, Adam took his free moral will and used it against God, thus severing the relationship between God and man.

It was never in God's will for man to know sickness, sin and death; but, when Adam rebelled in the Garden of Eden, Satan gained dominion over man. From then on, the door was open for the enemy to steal everything that God intended for us to have—including our relationship with Him.

When our communion with God was severed, we lost not only our pure, sincere mind toward God, but the knowledge of how to handle a relationship with Him!

Fear, doubt, unbelief, and mistrust of God rushed in to fill the place where revelation, wisdom, and knowledge of Him was intended to be. Darkness came to eat away at the very core of our beings. Envy, pride, jealousy, and hatred not only destroyed us, but blinded us to the knowledge of His will.

The God we serve is a God of **purpose**, plan, design and objectivity. After man's fall from communion with Him, God has had one major objective: to reconcile man back to Himself in a powerful love relationship that is unequaled in the universe!

How passionately we can hear Him call out to us in His Word: *"I don't want your sacrifices—I want your love; I don't want your offerings—I want you to know me" (Hosea 6:6, TLB).*

Through the death and resurrection of His Son, God once more opened the way for us to have this kind of loving fellowship with Him. And for a brief time, the saints of the early Church did know Him in this way. As we have noted, they did not struggle with the question of knowing God's will...they just did it.

Then something happened to the Church. During the period of the Dark Ages, it entered a period of centralization...and organization. It lost its simplicity and became rich and worldly. The saints lost their single-minded walk in the Holy Spirit. They lost the faith that they were born in, and they began to live under a structure of man-made organization instead.

To sum it all up, they lost the experience of what it was like to live in union with God. To compensate for this, the Church began to manufacture Christians, and like anything else that is manufactured, the Church lost its life.

Today the Church is like the "prodigal son" who is just now deciding to come back to his intended "home."

In Luke, Chapter 15, there is a story of a wealthy father who gave his two sons their inheritance while he was still living.

One son went off into a far country, where he wasted all his money on riotous living. One day while he was hungry and suffering, reaping the pains of what he had sown, he found himself shoveling the muck, the mire, the slop, and the dirt to pigs in a pig pen.

In that condition, the Bible says the boy came to himself. He said, "Why do I stay here in this condition, when over in my father's house there is plenty and more to spare?"

What a parallel this is to the way Christians have been living! We have been sitting around in the muck and the mire, living so far below our heritage—so far below our stature and what has been provided for us.

The prodigal son said, "I will get up out of this pig pen and I will go to my father's house." And he did. He said, "I will throw myself down before my father." And he did. He said, "I will repent." And he did. He said, "I will ask forgiveness." And he did.

His father forgave him, called a great big feast in his honor. He said, "This my son was dead and is now alive. He has come back into his father's house to receive that which is available within his family."

God has purposed that this restoration phase of the harvest time cycle, all that is available in the family of God be restored to us. As the prophet Joel prophesied: *"So I will restore to you the years that the swarming locust has eaten, the crawling locust, the consuming locust, and the chewing locust, my great army which I sent among you. You shall eat in plenty and be satisfied, and praise the name of the LORD your God, who has dealt wondrously with you; and My people shall never be put to shame. Then you shall know that I am in the midst of Israel, and that I am the LORD your God and there is no other. My people shall never be put to shame. And it shall come to pass afterward that I will pour out My spirit on all flesh; your sons and your daughters shall prophesy, your old men shall dream dreams, your young men shall see visions; and also on My menservants and on My maidservants I will pour out My Spirit in those days" (Joel 2:25-29, NKJ).*

But, the greatest thing that will be restored to you during this cycle is knowledge of the character of God Himself. This is the first prerequisite to being continually in tune with His will. Why?

Because God's character is what motivates His will! You will come to know His will in every situation because you have come to increasingly know the character behind (and of) that will.

We see the parallel to this in an earthly marriage. If you ask my wife, Theresa, (who has been married to me for over 50 years) what type of food I prefer, or what I would like to do on a vacation, she can tell you immediately what my choice would be. Why? Because she knows me! And since she knows my nature, she has developed a "sixth sense" for what I desire in almost every situation.

Now, you may be thinking that this all sounds quite feasible in a human relationship, but how do you ever develop that "sixth sense" with God?

The truth is that He has already started this process within you. When did He do it? The moment you were born again in His Son. That very day when you came to the foot of the cross and cried out, "Lord, help me! I give my life to You." God placed the seed of His Son within your innermost being.

The miracle of it is that contained in this seed of His Son within you, God has given you everything you need to come into full, intimate knowledge and fellowship with Him. You need only to learn how to get in touch with it. For He has given you everything you need to learn to discern, understand, grasp and put into action His perfect will for your life.

The Apostle Paul writes: *"Therefore, if anyone is in Christ, he is a new creation; old things have passed away; behold, all things have become new" (II Corinthians 5:17, NKJ).*

Already He has given you: *"...all things that (**are requisite and suited**) to life and godliness, through the (**full, personal**) knowledge of Him..." (II Peter 1:3, TAB).*

This does not mean that being restored into greater communion with God is instantaneous! Quite the contrary, it is a growth process in which, as you exercise what He has given you, true fellowship will begin to unfold.

Neither does it mean that suddenly you will begin seeing the entire plan for your life spread out before you. Nor will you always know why God is leading you down one path instead of another. For many of His ways (and His reasons) are beyond our knowing! (See *Isaiah 55:8-9*).

What it does mean is that gently, day by day, you will begin to experience that "still, small voice" of the Holy Spirit within your heart saying, "Turn here. Stop there. You're doing fine. I'm with you."

Again, this is a growth process. And, no one understands growing up as well as your heavenly Father does. Just as no earthly father would expect his one-year-old child to play football, or his four-year-old to drive a car, your Father does not expect you to commune with Him on a level of spiritual adulthood when you are only six months old in the Lord!

Upon hearing this, people will often ask me, "Brother Cerullo, are you saying that there is a 'perfect' and a 'permissive' will of God, and that we are not expected to know the perfect will of God when we are only babies in the Lord?"

My answer is that God's will is always His perfect will...period!

He will never ask more of us than we can handle at our stage of growth. Nor will He ever expect us to be responsible for anything that is beyond our level of communion with Him. His will for us is perfect no matter what stage of development we are in.

However, as we are growing we sometimes mistake our own, self-inspired course of action for His will because we have not taken the time to truly wait on Him or seek His direction. Thus, what people often refer to as the "permissive'' will of God is actually their own self-will which they have put into operation, and God has chosen (at that time) not to interfere.

As in the case of the prodigal son, this state will not go on forever. Sooner or later, they will feel God prodding them back on the track. Then it is up to each individual whether to comply or to rebel.

Those who choose to join with Him will discover that they are increasingly able to detect and resist their own wills and to walk more and more in step with His perfect will.

At this point, you may be wondering, "Well, if all Spirit-filled Christians have the seed of God within them, and are supposed to be growing, why is the Church today still in such confusion and despair concerning His will? Why do millions of 'born-again' Christians feel unable to get in touch with Him? What does it take to be restored to experience His new life within us?"

The answer lies in one sentence, dramatically revealed to us by the Apostle Paul. He said, *"...be transformed (**changed**) by the (**entire**) renewal of your mind..." (Romans 12:2, TAB).*

This renewal of your mind is the **gateway** to a new, vital relationship with the living God Himself. And, it is the **key** that unlocks the knowledge of His will for your life.

Chapter 2

Unleash the power of your renewed mind!

*"Do not be conformed to this world—this age, fashioned after and adapted to its external, superficial customs. But be transformed (**changed**) by the (**entire**) renewal of your mind—by its new ideals and its new attitude—so that you may prove (**for yourselves**) what is the good and acceptable and perfect will of God, even the thing which is good and acceptable and perfect (**in His sight for you**)" (Romans 12:2, TAB).*

I f the Apostle Paul is telling us that the key to the transformation from your old nature into new life in Christ is the renewal of your mind, just what does he mean by "renew"?

According to the dictionary, to renew means "to make like new; to restore to freshness, vigor, or perfection; to make new spiritually; to rebuild, replace and replenish." Now, can you imagine all this happening to your mind?

Can you conceive of your very thought processes, your attitudes towards people, the plans for your life, and your entire perspective on God being transformed into something new?

As amazing as it may sound, this is exactly what God yearns to do for you. Why?

Because your old, unrenewed (or carnal) mind is incapable of coming into true communion with Him!

In fact, it isn't capable of ever really comprehending, experiencing, or laying hold of the true things of God. As the Apostle Paul so adamantly states: *"...the Spirit searches all things, yes, the deep things of God. For what man knows the things of a man except the spirit of the man which is in him? Even so no one knows the things of God except the Spirit of God...But the natural man does not receive the things of the Spirit of God, for they are foolishness to him; nor can he know them, because they are spiritually discerned" (I Corinthians 2:10-11,14, NKJ).*

What has happened today is that thousands of sincere Christians are engaged in deep, painful struggles to determine God's will because they are striving to understand and receive the things of God with their natural minds, and this is impossible!

How it grieves me to see so many of God's people lost in turmoil and confusion, because they are trying to "figure out" God's will with the tools of their natural understanding. No one has ever told them that no amount of human reasoning, human imagination, calculating, seeking, or probing into "head knowledge" of God can ever appropriate the life, experience, and true understanding of God Himself, much less receive revelation of His will.

The Apostle Paul has told us, *"...we have the mind of Christ" (I Corinthians 2:16).* But only with the power of the Holy Spirit (the renewed Spirit of our mind) can we ever get in touch with the mind of Christ within us to unleash its power and its mysteries.

What must we do to renew our minds in the Spirit of God?

According to the Amplified translation of *Romans 12:2*, the renewal of our minds is intrinsically connected to a change in our attitudes and our ideals. But what is it that **shapes** our attitudes and ideals?

Build a new inner vision

We form our beliefs and attitudes based on how we see people and events around us. But the most important image, the image which controls and directs the way in which we see everything else, is the image we have of ourselves.

It is how we see ourselves which determines the thoughts we allow ourselves to think, thus forming the attitudes which change our lives for better or for worse.

If, for instance, we do not see that victory and progress are possible in our Christian lives, we will never believe that we can become overcomers!

That is why the Word of God stresses: *"...be constantly renewed in the spirit of your mind—having a fresh mental and spiritual attitude; And put on the new nature...created in God's image..." (Ephesians 4:23-24, TAB).*

It is the way in which we visualize ourselves which motivates the way we act. And these actions, in turn, reinforce the image we have of ourselves, making it even stronger.

Yet, this new view of yourself as someone walking in obedience to His Word is not one of your old "self" (or old nature) suddenly being repaired and repainted for Jesus. No. What you are now visualizing is a totally new person, springing forth from deep within your innermost being, empowered and patterned after Christ Himself. As Paul says: *"...it is no longer I who live, but Christ lives in me..." (Galatians 2:20, NKJ).*

Thus, it is through building a new inner vision of seeing yourself as God sees you—and acting on it—which will be the bridge between your old, unrenewed mind, and a mind that has been restored in the image of God; a mind capable of receiving and comprehending His thoughts.

God tells us that: *"...as he (Jesus) is, so are we in this world" (I John 4:17).* But, how many of us see ourselves as our Lord is? Most of us have no trouble imagining that we will be like Him someday "when we get to heaven," but how many of us see ourselves as being (and **acting**) like him here and now?

Yet, it is this failure in our willingness to see ourselves as God sees us that has the Church in a terrible rut. For, when we don't see ourselves as being like Him, we take on the attitude of being powerless. Being powerless, we fail to act as He would act. Thus, the revelation power of God is blocked from getting through to us...and the world!

Whenever our self-image remains "stuck" in the limited view of what we have always been in our old natures, we fall down in communion with God and in appropriating what is His perfect will for us to have.

But, praise God, He has provided us with a way to break through the bondage of all our old ways of thinking, into the new light of His revelation power!

We are going to be talking a great deal about revelation, and some of you may be wondering, "Brother Cerullo, what exactly is 'revelation'?"

Our definition of revelation is the "drawing away of the veil of darkness."

It is the stripping away of all the lies that Satan has told you about who you are.

It is the dissolution of all the preconceived ideas about your limitations, based on a self-image formed in your old life without Christ.

Revelation is the lifting of the veil and the dissolving of all darkness concerning His will for you as a new person in Him! And, revelation is power!

The Word of God tells us: *"Where there is no vision, the people perish..." (Proverbs 29:18).*

Now, are you ready for a bombshell?

The translators of the New King James version of the Bible interpret the word "vision" to mean revelation. So that translation reads: "Where there is no **revelation**, the people cast off restraint."

The Hebrew root of the word "vision" (or revelation) is "chazown," which means "to gaze at, mentally to perceive..."

The root for the word "perish" means "to become lawless." In other words, to step out of the will of God!

When we put it all together, God is telling us that without a new inner vision...or revelation...we are in grave danger of casting off all restraint, i.e., going out of His will.

With a new vision, there is new life like we have never thought possible before!

Chapter 3

See yourself as God sees you

"...it pleased God, who separated me from my mother's womb and called me through His grace, to reveal His Son in me..." (Galatians 1:15-16, NKJ).

One dark, stormy night, a boat in which the disciples were traveling was suddenly battered by a vicious storm. In utter panic, they screamed to the Lord, "Save us! We are perishing!" But instead of being sympathetic, Jesus sternly rebuked them for having little faith! *(Matthew 8:23-27)*.

Why? Weren't the winds and the waves real?

Of course they were...in the natural. But what was going on in the spirit world? How did the disciples fail the Lord? Let's take a look.

We can presume that by getting into the boat and instructing them to go to the other side of the lake, Jesus had already made the will of the Father known to the twelve. They were to set out for their destination and arrive there safely. They were not to die...they had work to do.

However, as soon as Satan used adverse weather conditions against them, they immediately lost their perspective of who

they were and what God's will was for them. Although the
Lord had already given them all power over the enemy, in
the turmoil of the storm they lost all vision of themselves
as men with spiritual authority. Instead of laying hold of the
new image of themselves in Him, they reverted to doubt and
fear.

Surely, at this point in their lives, the apostles had no
conception of the job ahead of them, or of the powerful role
they would play in the building of Christ's Church. But in
the stage they were at in the boat, God wanted them to act
on the small revelation He had already given them.

He wanted them to grasp a new inner vision of themselves,
which He was imparting to them. Then He wanted them to
build on it by acting on His Word.

This is always the way God works. First, He gives us small
revelations of His will for us. Then, by acting on these small
things, we loose Him to pour even greater revelations into
our hearts.

That dark night in the boat, the disciples did not
understand this. But centuries before them, a man named
Abraham did. He understood the significance, the power and
the importance of the new inner vision which God was
building in him, and he was willing to act on it. Thus, he
became the "father of faith."

We see an example of his interactions with God
dramatically illustrated in the 15th chapter of the book of
Genesis.

One night God took Abram (Abraham) outside and showed
him the stars. As soon as Abram had a clear picture of them
in his mind, God told him, *"So shall your descendants be"
(Genesis 15:5, TAB).*

A few years later (when Abraham had made the appropriate
sacrifices), God showed him a further vision of how his
descendants would be oppressed in Egypt for 400 years.

However, going on to Genesis 22, we see how God tested
Abraham's belief in the revelation he already had, by asking
him to sacrifice his own son, Isaac.

Please understand that it was not just Abraham's obedience
to God that was being tried; it was also his obedience to God's
Word, his faith in God's promise that he would have many
descendants.

Ultimately, it was his faith in that vision and his willingness to act on it that brought him into a realm of even greater revelation from God! For Abraham firmly believed without a doubt that even if Isaac were slain, God would resurrect him to fulfill His Word.

It was after Abraham took the step of action that God gave him the rest of the revelation concerning his offspring.

It was then that God said: *"...and your descendants shall possess the gate of their enemies. In your seed all nations of the earth shall be blessed, because you have obeyed My voice"* (Genesis 22:17-18, TAB).

Do you see how the revelation of God's will came to Abraham in several stages? First, God spoke. Then Abraham acted on what he knew and offered animal sacrifices. God then gave him another vision.

Next, Abraham took a giant step of obedience (and faith) and God rewarded him with another, more powerful revelation.

Thus, the bond between them grew stronger and deeper with each step of obedience on Abraham's part!

Tragically, in contrast to this, the children of Israel later failed to enter into the Promised Land, because they refused to act on what they knew to be God's promise, and this kind of inner rebellion was counted as unbelief. Thus, God would take them no further than they were willing to go in faith.

We can see from this that we set our own limits on how far God can take us! Please take a moment right now to evaluate your life. How far you are willing to go with God will greatly determine how much of His will He will reveal to you!

Did you know that every promise in His Word holds the seed of a miraculous change in your life...which is God's will for you!

Yes, it is by changing your attitude toward His promises to you and by building a new inner vision based on them, that your mind will be renewed and you will be transformed into the likeness of His Son!

The Apostle Peter tells us: *"...He has bestowed on us His precious and exceedingly great promises, so that through them you...become sharers (**partakers**) of the divine nature"* (II Peter 1:4, TAB).

Are you ready to take your first step into this new dimension of revelation?

Let us begin now to go step by step into the will of God. Step 1 is to find yourself in the Word of God.

Chapter 4

Step 1
Find yourself in
the Word of God

"...we all, with unveiled face, beholding as in a mirror the glory of the Lord, are being transformed into the same image from glory to glory..." (II Corinthians 3:18, NKJ).

Recently, one of my staff members told about a conversation her seven-year-old son had with his teacher. The teacher asked the boy what he wanted to be when he grew up. He replied, "An artist."

She said, "Why do you want to be an artist?"

"Because my Mom's one."

"How are you going to go about becoming an artist?"

"By watching my Mom."

This is how human beings grow up to be like their parents. From the time an infant is old enough to focus his eyes, he watches every move his parents make. He then begins to imitate what he sees.

This, in a nutshell, is exactly how God intends for us to "go about" becoming His full-grown sons: by watching and imitating Him! From there we can go on to be participators in His life!

Jesus testified: *"Most assuredly, I say to you, the Son can do nothing of Himself, but what He sees the Father do; for whatever He does, the Son also does in like manner" (John 5:19, NKJ).*

Just how do we "watch" every move our heavenly Father makes? We begin by finding ourselves in the Word of God.

Right now, no matter what trying situation or circumstance you may be facing, sit down and open your Bible. Ask the Holy Spirit to help you find someone in the Bible who went through the same thing, or to direct you to a passage that deals with your particular condition.

Do you have difficulty finding "quiet time" to be alone with the Lord? Ask yourself, "What did the great prophets do? What did David do? What did Jesus do?"

These people victoriously overcame their circumstances by arising early in the morning to worship God and let Him speak to them! (*Psalm 5:3, Isaiah 50:4,* and *Luke 4:42.*)

Can you see yourself doing the same thing? Ask the Holy Spirit to move on your mind until you do, then build on this new vision of yourself by actively getting up an hour early or setting aside a special "quiet time" alone with God.

Is your problem financial? If it is, perhaps the Lord will direct you to the passage that says: *"Give and it will be given to you: good measure, pressed down, shaken together, and running over will be put into your bosom. For with the same measure that you use, it will be measured back to you" (Luke 6:38, NKJ).*

Can you see yourself giving when you're down to your last dollar? Maybe not. Yet, this is exactly what the Word of God says to do.

Currently, you may be in despair and asking yourself, "Is it God's will that I be buried in bills?"

No. But it is His will that you obey His Word to get out of it, no matter how impossible His solution may seem to your natural, unrenewed mind.

Although the bills may seem horrendous to you now, God wants to use your current situation to lead you into a new realm of miracle thinking; a realm in which your natural mind will no longer hinder you from appropriating all He has in store for you.

This entire process of visualizing yourself as a new person

acting in line with His Word may feel uncomfortable and silly at first, perhaps even a little frightening. But imagine how Peter must have felt when the Lord told him to go get his tax money out of the mouth of a fish!

Can you see yourself obediently acting on that? Yet, through that exercise the Lord was training Peter to trust God and to believe Him for even greater things later on.

Make no mistake, you are not the one who is creating these miracles, or bringing about the remarkable transformation in yourself through your thinking. It is God Who is doing the work.

All you are doing is agreeing to let go of the old image of yourself by yielding to His blueprint of who you really are (based on His Word). Then God, the Master Builder, takes over and with His power makes you into the person He desires you to be according to His will, not yours. He is always the Source of any change in you...not the power of your own thinking. But through your thoughts you give Him permission to work.

Let's try another example of yielding to His blueprint. Is there anyone in your office or family with whom you just cannot get along, no matter how hard you try? Someone who is constantly degrading you or making unreasonable demands?

If there is, can you imagine yourself obeying God's Word which says: *"...whoever desires to become great among you, let him be your servant. And whoever desires to be first among you, let him be your slave—"* (Matthew 20:26-27, NKJ), or *"...If someone demands your coat, give him your shirt besides. Give what you have to anyone who asks you for it...Love your enemies!...Lend to them! And don't be concerned about the fact that they won't repay..."* (Luke 6:29-30,35, TLB).

Can you see yourself as a humble servant to those who despise you? Or, in your heart do you cry out, "Dear God, is it Your will that I be constantly oppressed by these people? Don't You want me somewhere else?"

Perhaps "down the road" He does want you to work or live somewhere else, but for now He wants you to come into complete obedience right where you are! In His timing He will move you on to greater service in Him, not before.

Just the idea of visualizing yourself as being humble, loving, or giving to your enemies under the stressful conditions may seem extremely difficult. But, praise God, you don't have to carry out this new behavior in your own power!

Once you agree to God's will in your situation by finding yourself and then seeing yourself in His Word, the Holy Spirit will empower you to take that crucial step of obedience!

You will begin to see yourself as God sees you.

However, I must warn you that the first few times you attempt this step of finding (and seeing) yourself in God's Word, you may encounter a tremendous battle between your flesh and your spirit.

Why? Because although your intentions are good, there is still part of you that is unsurrendered to that particular aspect of God's will.

For instance, if the Word clearly indicates that you go to a brother and forgive him for some offense, but you cannot possibly see yourself doing anything like that, there is some aspect of unforgiveness in your nature which is still unyielded to God.

Being able to visualize yourself as acting in a certain manner is a sure sign that you have accepted that behavior...and that you have surrendered that area to God. However, not being able to visualize it is a sure sign that you have not yet fully accepted it in your heart.

Whenever I hear someone say, "Brother Cerullo, I know what God's Word says, but I just cannot see myself doing that right now," I know that it is time to proceed to Step 2 in our journey: That step is the conscious surrender of your will in that area of your life.

Chapter 5

Step 2
Surrender
your will

*"I appeal to you therefore, brethren, and beg of you in view of (**all**) the mercies of God, to make a decisive dedication of your bodies—presenting all your members and faculties—as a living sacrifice, holy (**devoted, consecrated**) and well pleasing to God, which is your reasonable (**rational, intelligent**) service and spiritual worship" (Romans 12:1, TAB).*

One day I heard a story which vividly illustrates the subtle trap into which many of us fall when we seek God's will in adverse circumstances.

The story involved a young lady who was newly born again and very fervent in the Lord, but whose family was backslidden. Her parents resented her new-found commitment and made life at home quite miserable.

Naturally, her first reaction was that she wanted to move out, but she told her prayer group that she first desired to know God's will about where she should go.

When the group interceded for her, several members confirmed that it was God's will for her to remain at home a while longer in order to develop a humbler, more loving attitude toward her family. God would then use the transformation in her as a mighty witness to change the hearts of her parents.

Her immediate reaction to this counsel was typical of the way so many of us respond. She said, "That could never happen...not with them!"

With this attitude, she became barricaded in her own limited vision of what God could (and wanted) to do, although she continued to tell her friends, "I want to do God's will. Please pray about where He wants me to go."

What happened was that she did not want to know God's will in this situation. She wanted His approval of her own will, while she kept that part of her heart unyielded to Him. Her prayers became consumed with trying to get an okay from God for what she wanted to do!

When this was pointed out, she said, "Oh, I surrendered my heart to Jesus when I was saved. He knows I'm His."

Beloved, it is true that each one of us did sincerely yield our hearts to God on that day of salvation. We asked Him to rule and reign in our hearts from then on...and we meant it.

Then our first opportunity for forgiveness came along, and we passed it up...choosing instead to get back on the throne of that one little portion of our hearts.

Next came another chance to help a brother carry a painful burden...and we passed that up, because we were "too busy." Back we were on the throne of another little portion of our hearts.

And so it went, until we were merrily back in control of every aspect of our lives...fueled by all the selfish thoughts and habits of our old ways and our old nature, deceiving ourselves into thinking that we were surrendered to the Lord!

In reality, it was not the Holy Spirit Who was in control, but the carnal mind. The carnal mind is incapable of putting its trust in God. It is incapable of being empowered by God. It can only force us to focus on circumstances, keep us feeding on circumstances, and hold us in bondage to them!

As a result, a battle soon rages in our minds...the battle of looking to circumstances versus exercising the new faith of God within us. It is during these battles that we discover that our minds and our wills are not as surrendered to God as we thought they were, and that true surrender is not a "one-time" decision when we were saved.

We learn that it is an active process of making minute-by-minute decisions in favor of God; of choosing to exercise our faith in Him every day and every hour of our lives.

Increasingly, with each day of new growth in the Lord, we become more aware of parts of ourselves that we may be trying to hold on to. These "hidden hold-outs" put up barriers between ourselves and God, and force us to rely on our carnal thinking (based on circumstances), not the renewed, Spirit-empowered mind of Christ.

You are not alone!

You are not alone in your struggles with the surrender of your will in those painful little pockets of your heart. One of the greatest men in the Bible went through the same thing, and as a result of his surrender, there came a spiritual breakthrough that changed the entire course of God's people.

That breakthrough came when Jacob, the schemer, the trickster, the conniver, finally surrendered his will to God. It was through his action of surrender that God ordained that he was no longer Jacob the manipulator. He was now Israel, a prince who had power with God and with men! *(Genesis 32:28).*

At this point we may ask ourselves just what it was about Jacob's surrender that so touched the heart of God.

Let's take a look at this story of Jacob as it relates to the victory God wants to bring into your heart, your mind and your will.

The book of Genesis tells us that for 21 years Jacob lived in torment away from his real home because he had extorted his older brother Esau's birthright. Esau had vowed that he would kill Jacob for this. In fear, Jacob fled to a land called Haran.

Then, one day God communicated his divine will to Jacob. He told him, *"Return to the land of your father and to your people, and I will be with you"* (Genesis 31:3, TAB).

Notice that with the revelation of His will, God provided Jacob with the promise that He would be with him...that is, Jacob would have everything he needed to carry out God's instructions.

By telling Jacob, "I will be with you," God was actually saying, "If you will obey the word that I give you, I will deal well with you. I will protect and keep you. I will see you through."

Beloved, God doesn't operate any differently with you than He did with Jacob. It is so essential that you, like Jacob, not only obey God's voice, but believe that with the declaration of His will, God will give you every single thing you need to carry it out!

Jacob understood this, and in obedience to what he knew was the will of God, he set out with his family for "home." However, dark circumstances soon intervened when he heard that his brother, Esau, was coming!

Immediately, Jacob forgot all about the promise of God's protection that came with His will, and retreated into his old way of fearful, defensive thinking. Seeing himself as a fugitive, he thought, "Oh, I know Esau is coming to kill me. I had better take action to save what I can."

Fear dominated his thoughts. No longer could he see himself trusting God no matter what the circumstances. No longer could he see himself as being divinely protected by God no matter what enemies appeared on the horizon. All he could see was trouble! He was blinded into thinking that all he had was himself to rely on.

He said, "I will organize my people into three droves...one, two, three. I will split them all up. The first one will meet Esau and his 400 mighty men. They will fall down before him and say, 'All of these gifts...cattle, donkeys and so on are from your servant Jacob.' They will fall down and compromise before Esau." Then Jacob said, "When he kills them, then he will meet the second band. When he kills the second band, he will meet the third band, then I will be there."

What a morbid outlook, but the person who feels he only has himself to rely on is bound to think that way.

Just when Jacob was about to create his own defeat through negative thinking and schemes of his own mind, God dramatically intervened. He sent an angel who wrestled with him all night, until the break of day *(Genesis 32:25-26)*.

At that point, something dramatic happened to this conniver that changed his life. What was it? What was it that transformed Jacob the manipulator into Israel, the prince of power with men and with God?

What happened was a total change in Jacob's position

regarding his relationship with God.

When the wrestling match began, Jacob saw himself in a position of natural strength and power. However, when the angel finally touched his thigh and crippled him, Jacob could no longer contend with God from his old position of natural strength. He could only cling to Him!

Suddenly he could only cry out in total dependency, "I will not let thee go."

This was what God had been waiting for! And it was Jacob's finally surrendering to a new position of clinging to and relying entirely on God that then allowed God to take the spiritual blindness from his eyes and let him see himself as God saw him...forgiven, renewed, strengthened and with the position of a prince in the spirit realm! A prince with God and with men.

Yes, with his surrender and yieldedness to God came Jacob's greatest victory!

In the next scene we no longer see a scheming, manipulating man fearfully running out of the will of God. Instead, we find Jacob marching out to meet Esau in the full confidence that God's will was his and that God was fully on his side!

It was then that he discovered that Esau wasn't coming to kill him, he was coming to forgive him! God had already gone before Jacob and mellowed Esau's heart.

God wants you to have the same breakthrough into surrender that Jacob had. No longer does your heavenly Father want you to react to circumstances in the power of your natural mind. From now on, your circumstances are to be met with the mind and the will of God which will be imparted to your mind by the Holy Spirit as you take each step of surrender in even the tiniest areas of your life!

This brings us to a question that I am asked quite frequently: "Do adverse circumstances mean that I am out of the will of God?"

No. Most likely, trying situations mean that God is giving you a tremendous opportunity to overcome your circumstances in His will, with the weapons He has provided. Therefore, He may choose not to take you out of difficulties, but to bring you victoriously through them to prove Himself!

You are not to take a back seat to Satan. You are not to watch the devil "do his thing" and say, "Oh well, it must have been God's will!" Remember, there are no great victories without great battles.

God's will is for His people to be **overcomers**! And an army of overcomers He will have! We are to be on the offensive, not the defensive.

There is one more aspect of this subject of circumstances which we must consider. Just as negative (or adverse) circumstances do not necessarily reflect God's will, we also must be very careful not to take positive circumstances as a "green light" or a "sign" that we should proceed with a plan that looks good to us. Sometimes it is more difficult to surrender our brilliant, positive ideas than it is our negative ones!

Remember that God's ultimate purpose is for us to come into communion with Him.

This means that we must cling to Him for guidance when things look good, as well as when they look bad.

The journeys of Paul are a perfect example. In *Acts 16:6-7,* Paul and his companions set out to evangelize the mission field of Asia. Yet, when he reached Phrygia and the region of Galatia, they were forbidden by the Holy Spirit to preach the Word in Asia. After they had come to Mysia, they tried to go into Bithynia, but the Spirit did not permit them.

To Paul's natural mind, the setting must have looked perfect for what he was called to do. After all, there were countless lost souls who were completely unevangelized; he was already there, and his talents certainly would have been useful!

Yet, for reasons known only to God, the Spirit said "**no**."

Fortunately, Paul's will was surrendered to the Spirit of God. He was willing to look past his own thinking and press on to Troas where he received a fuller vision of God's will for his ministry.

The entire time that God was leading him on his journey, there were many places that Paul could have stepped out of the will of God by saying, "This town looks great. Look at all the needs. It must be where I'm supposed to be!"

How many times Satan must have tempted him to settle down and open a ministry in the wrong place at the wrong time. But Paul continued to seek God for confirmation of His will. Each step of the way he continued to ask God if what looked obvious to his natural mind really was God's plan.

At each stop, Paul was willing to say "**no!**" to his own thoughts and plans and listen to God! It's a good thing he did, for how could he have possibly dreamed that God was leading him to Greece.

I myself have experienced what Paul must have felt as he surrendered plans which looked so good, so perfect.

As a young man I knew that God had called me as an evangelist. At the age of fifteen, I was already holding meetings in auditoriums, in high schools, and Youth for Christ meetings. When I graduated from Bible College I knew that God had called me to great things.

What I didn't know was that as one of my challenges, He was also calling me to pastor what must have been the smallest church in the world!

You know, I never could picture myself speaking to only 40 people every Sunday. When I received the offer, I almost fell on the floor laughing.

Then God got hold of me.

He revealed to me that this offer was in His will, and I was to take it.

Not only did I have to change my thinking about my sudden change in status (the church members had even run the last pastor out of town), but it required some deep yielding of my heart in that area.

Theresa and I were just about to be married. We didn't have a car and I had only $35 to my name. Now here we were accepting the pastorate of the tiniest church in New England.

When I started in that church, the testimony of the Christians in that town was unbelievably bad. In fact, one of the first things I did was to tear up all their membership cards and put them all on probation!

But, because I remained completely surrendered to God no matter what the situation looked like, God did phenomenal things in that little congregation. We became instruments of a great revival that reverberated throughout New England.

Stop for a few moments and reflect on your own life. What is the deep, hidden area where you need God's help the most? Is it in your ministry for Him...your finances...your marriage...your relationship with your children...your relationship with people in your church?

Whatever it is, ask the Holy Spirit to beam His big floodlight into your heart and show you what you may need surrendered to God. In what specific area of your life can you yield your will to Him now, so that a new revelation of His will may flood that pocket of your innermost being?

In what aspect of your life can you begin now to stop relying on your own thoughts and plans, and begin to cling to Him as you have never done before?

The Lord assures you that if you will trust in the Lord with all thine heart; lean not unto thine own understanding and in all thy ways acknowledge Him, He shall direct thy paths *(Proverbs 3:5-6)*. And if you will commit thy way unto the Lord; trusting also in Him; He shall bring it to pass *(Psalm 37:5)*.

God is waiting for you to cry out to Him. He longs for you to say, "Father, I surrender. I turn my back on the thoughts, limitations and self-image of my natural mind regarding this situation. I surrender my will to You on a new level. From now on, I will begin to see myself as You see me; to act, to obey Your Word in this matter, and trust You to bring it to pass. "Father, no longer do I want to be a child of Yours in name only. As I yield my life to You on a new level, the eyes of my understanding are being opened. The veil of darkness is being lifted. I am beginning to experience the rich fellowship of Your guidance! I am beginning to see a new life for myself in Your perfect will."

Chapter 6

Step 3
Make love of God
your first priority

"And you shall love the LORD your God with all your heart, with all your soul, with all your mind, and with all your strength" (Mark 12:30, NKJ).

When we began to explore the steps into greater communion with God, we noted that the key to coming into knowledge of His will lies in the renewal of our minds... in "its new ideals and its new attitude."

This entire matter of forming new ideals so dramatically shapes our thought lives that it comprises Step 3 of our study, which is, Make Love of God Your First Priority.

To begin with, exactly what is an "ideal"?

An ideal is a model we hold in our mind as a standard to imitate. In other words, ideals are the standards we reach for; they are what determine our priorities in life.

Our ideals are extremely powerful because what we love, desire and focus our attention on is what we become. For instance, if we hold the things of this world or the world's standard of success as our ideal, we will become like those in the world whom we are imitating.

If we hold our Lord as our ideal, we will focus continually on Him until we start thinking as He would think; acting as He would act.

Satan has led many of God's children into the bondage of their own self-natures and to the world, by enticing them into setting their love and desires (what the Bible calls "affections") on the world's ideals of success and prosperity...not God's. He has distracted God's children away from making the things of God their number one priority.

Throughout our entire journey into knowing God and His will, there is one major pitfall which each one of us will have to persistently guard against, that is the pitfall of letting our minds slip into the wrong ideals. When we desire the wrong things and God Himself is no longer the first priority in our lives, we are headed for trouble.

As the Apostle Paul tells us: *"...seek those things which are above, where Christ sitteth on the right hand of God. **Set your affection on things above,** not on things on the earth" (Colossians 3:1-2).*

I know that many of you are probably thinking, "Is Brother Cerullo saying that it isn't God's will for me to be prosperous?"

No, I'm not saying that.

What I am saying is that it is wrong for you to set your affections (and priorities) on the things of this world and to never move on to desiring the true success (and prosperity) of the Kingdom of God! If you could only realize how tragic it is to spend your precious time in this life attaining (or worrying about) the world's perishable "riches" and not concentrating on the spiritual riches God longs so much to give you.

God has promised us that He *"will liberally supply...your every need according to His riches in glory in Christ Jesus"* (Philippians 4:19, TAB).

Notice that He says He will supply everything we need. What are our needs?

We know that we need food and clothing and these types of things. But it is for Christ's people to look beyond that...

Look beyond it to what?

We must look beyond to His riches in Christ Jesus...to the riches through which our material needs will be met, if only we will concentrate on attaining the spiritual riches first!

Just what are our riches in Christ Jesus?

Throughout the Word, we see that they include the riches of His love; His wisdom; His mercy, faith, kindness, understanding; and knowledge of Himself.

For a long time we have been stuck in a spiritual rut of not growing or coming into these riches, because we have had our eyes and affections set on things that are temporal. We have been saying, "Praise God. He is going to bless me! Hallelujah, I'll have that new Cadillac or boat."

The basic teaching has been to have the faith to get things. To have the faith to walk around as an heir of God and say, "Bless God. I have everything. All the world's riches belong to me."

God is taking you beyond that. He is telling you now that there is so much more He wants you to seek Him for than the temporal things of this world. He wants you to refocus your desires; to reset your priorities; and make your number one priority seeking Him and His riches.

Remember that the Spirit of God is in you. He is there, dwelling within your heart for many purposes, but one major purpose is to bring you into a revelation and understanding of God's will and the "mysteries" of His plan; mysteries which He has hidden in Himself throughout the ages.

Right now, in this restoration phase of the harvest time cycle, we are entering into the full possibility and potentiality of being in a spiritual relationship with Him that is so deep...so strong...so powerful, that we will actually begin to zero in on all that God has for man!

The time has come when each one of us (who sincerely wants a relationship with God in a new spiritual dimension), will have to evaluate the true desires and priorities of our hearts.

Each one of us is now being called to courageously face the question, "Am I living for myself or for Him?"

The Apostle Paul faced this question squarely when he said, *"...He died for all, that those who live should live no longer for themselves, but for Him who died for them and rose again" (II Corinthians 5:15, NKJ).*

Why are we placing so much emphasis on setting our love, affections and priorities squarely on God?

Because the knowledge and the power that you will need to be a true overcomer in the heat of trials and battles can only be appropriated through a deeply rooted love relationship with Him. These roots do not develop overnight. They grow day by day as you learn to set all your desires on the things of God.

The Apostle Paul knew this and was a vivid example of someone who, because his priorities were right, was able to be more than a conqueror over all that could come against him.

The priorities of Paul

Let's take a look at Paul. First of all, what does he himself state is his number one priority? In the book of Philippians, he tells us: *"(For my determined purpose is) that I may know Him—that I may progressively become more deeply and intimately acquainted with Him, perceiving and recognizing and understanding (the wonders of His Person) more strongly and more clearly..."* (Philippians 3:10, TAB).

Does this mean that Paul was so close to God that his life was trouble-free?

Absolutely not! To the contrary, he loved the Lord so much that he gloried in sharing the sufferings of Christ. He even prayed: *"...that I may in that same way come to know the power outflowing from His resurrection...and that I may so share His sufferings as to be continually transformed (in spirit) into His likeness..."* (Philippians 3:10, TAB).

Perhaps no human being on the face of this earth (with the exception of our Lord) ever suffered more for the Church than Paul. As he himself testified: *"I have worked harder, been put in jail oftener, been whipped times without number, and faced death again and again and again. Five different times the Jews gave me their terrible thirty-nine lashes. Three times I was beaten with rods. Once I was stoned. Three times I was shipwrecked...I have traveled many weary miles...I have lived with weariness and pain and sleepless nights..."* (II Corinthians 11:23-27 TLB).

His incredible roster of suffering and tribulation goes on and on. Yet, what was his attitude toward all this?

His focus—His priority relationship with our Lord—was so strong...so powerful...that he was able to say, *"But none of these things moved me"* (Acts 20:24).

He even called these afflictions "light" (II Corinthians 4:17).

From there he goes on to loudly proclaim his "secret of success" for keeping these brutal sufferings in such an astounding perspective. He says: *"...we look not at the things which are seen, but at the things which are not seen: for the things which are seen are temporal; but the things which are not seen are eternal" (II Corinthians 4:18).*

It was through keeping his mind steadfastly focused on God that Paul's reaction to the greatest testings was to victoriously declare, *"Who shall separate us from the love of Christ?" (Romans 8:35).*

Yes, Paul's amazing, unwavering attitude through all adversity was that *"...amid all these things we are more than conquerors and gain a surpassing victory through Him Who loved us" (Romans 8:37, TAB).*

Throughout the severest trials he did not complain, question, or murmur if this was God's will. Instead, he maintained an unwavering attitude of exalting the Almighty through his triumphant statement: *"For I am persuaded beyond doubt...that neither death, nor life, nor angels, nor principalities, nor things impending and threatening, nor things to come, nor powers, Nor height, nor depth, nor anything else in all creation will be able to separate us from the love of God which is in Christ Jesus our Lord" (Romans 8:38-39, TAB).*

What an example Paul is to us!

Can you see yourself reacting to affliction in the same way?

Can you see yourself singing praises to God through imprisonment and torture such as Paul and Silas did? *(Acts 16:25).*

It is entirely possible! Only deep love can motivate anyone to maintain this level of perseverance or to appropriate this depth of overcoming power!

What about Job?

At this point, many of you may be wondering about another man in the Bible who underwent different kinds of suffering than Paul. As one partner expressed it, "Brother Cerullo, I understand why Paul suffered. He was suffering because he was doing God's will and Satan didn't like it. But what about personal sufferings such as Job endured? Are these kinds of trials really God's will for my life? What about sickness and personal loss? Is He putting me through these things because I have lessons to learn?"

Ultimately, these are questions that only you and God can answer. But I can give you a fresh perspective on the book of Job that perhaps you haven't considered before...a perspective that I hope will greatly encourage you to press on to a more vibrant, living relationship with your Lord.

When we begin to think about the problems in our lives for which we don't have answers, each one of us is prone to look up and say, "God, why did this happen?" or "Did You really allow this to come into my life?"

For those of you who have lost precious loved ones through an automobile accident or through some terrible catastrophe in life, you must have wondered many times if God is the only Power Who has the absolute, total control of all the circumstances in this world.

Since many of you have deeply identified with Job at one time or another, let us take a look at this marvelous man, his life, and his relationship to God.

First of all, what kind of man was he? His very name means "afflicted one." When we begin to look at him, the first thing we understand about Job is that he was no ordinary man.

He was a profound scholar and intellectual. In his sphere of life, Job was highly honored. He had financial wealth and prosperity of the Lord, for which he continually acknowledged God.

God called Job "perfect," but this did not mean that he was sinless. He was not sinless. He was perfect in the sense that he was completely mature before God.

Remember that man lives in two worlds...the natural world and the spirit world. While Job was undergoing severe trials in the natural realm of his circumstances, there was a spiritual trial going on behind the scenes of which Job had no knowledge. This trial involved his relationship with God!

Job's troubles began in the spirit world when Satan marched into the throne room of God and tried to accuse him of the only weakness Satan thought God might possibly find in him.

In essence, what Satan said to God was, *"Job's relationship with You is worth nothing. He worships You only for what You give him. Take away everything he has and he will curse You to Your face!" (Job 1:9-11).*

Notice that God was not trying Job...the enemy was. We will see how God permitted the trial of Job's faith for a very specific purpose, but He kept Satan on a very tight leash throughout the whole thing. Each step of the way God said to Satan, *"You can go so far with him and no further!" (Job 1:12, 2:6).*

How hard it is for us, as the children of God, to understand that in the very midst of our intense affliction, we can still be surrounded by the protection of God. If only we could understand that right in the middle of our worst times, we are still in the eye of God's love!

Job had no knowledge of this, but being an astounding man of patience, perseverance and endurance, he stood firm. When he lost his wealth he stood firm. When he lost his health he stood firm. When he lost his children, the love of his wife, and his friends, he stood firm saying, *"Though he slay me, yet will I trust in him" (Job 13:15).*

As we continue to read through Job's ordeal, we begin to see one of God's purposes for allowing this testing: that is, Job's relationship with Him was very limited!

It is amazing to observe that in all his bereavement, Job never once directly asked God to help him. Instead, Job's entire appeal was based on his own opinion of himself, that he was a righteous man who didn't deserve what was happening. He felt God owed him an explanation!

Although Job was the epitome of patient endurance, he was also tied up in his own self-righteousness. His eyes were glued to what he had done for God and on what God had done for him in the past. He had not yet developed a relationship which allowed him to fellowship with (or appeal to) God!

His entire inner vision...all the priorities of his mind...were "stuck" on what he felt he deserved based on the past. This is clearly expressed as we hear him cry out: *"Oh, that I were as in the months of old, as in the days when God watched over me" (Job 29:2, TAB).*

The image Job had in his mind was that all God wanted for him had already been fulfilled, and that it was all downhill from there. He had no further ideals or desires beyond what was. He never dreamed that one of God's purposes in allowing this trial of his faith was not to take away from him, but to bring Job into a new revelation of Himself where He could give him so much more.

Eventually, through Job's incredible endurance, God was able to break through to Job and bring him into this new revelation...a revelation which Job finally grasped.

Now we hear him saying: *"I had heard of You **(only)** by the hearing of the ear; but now my **(spiritual)** eye sees You. Therefore, I loathe **(my words)** and abhor myself, and repent in dust and ashes"* (Job 42:5-6, TAB).

Job was never the same again. He not only had head knowledge of His Creator, but a breakthrough in an experience of Him as well! At once, amazing things began to happen. As soon as Job received and grasped the revelation that God intended for him, Satan's time with him was over.

Yes, as soon as God had His way and His purposes were accomplished, the enemy had no more part with Job. It was then that *"the Lord blessed the latter days of Job more than his beginning"* (Job 42:12, TAB).

Who could have understood Job's trial when he was going through it? Surely not Job.

Who was in command? God!

Who won the victory in the end? God and Job together.

God loves you so much that in every instance He will stand with you through fiery trials to bring you (like Job) into a new revelation of your relationship with Him. (Also see *Isaiah 43:1-6*).

I know that many of you, like Job, are in desperate situations. But I also know that God loves you more than you can imagine. He wants to restore you to a new position in Him.

The only thing that can ruin you is quitting!

My prayer right now is that each of you will rise up and say to yourself and to the Lord: *"...I press on, that I may lay hold of that for which Christ Jesus has also laid hold of me...but one thing I do, forgetting those things which are behind and reaching forward to those things which are ahead, I press toward the goal for the prize of the upward call of God in Christ Jesus"* (Philippians 3:12-14, NKJ).

May you now be completely renewed and refreshed in your mind as you begin to put God first in everything you do. *"For none of us lives to himself, and no one dies to himself. For if we live, we live to the Lord; and if we die, we die to the Lord. Therefore, whether we live or die, we are the Lord's"* (Romans 14:7-8, NKJ).

Chapter 7

Step 4
Put on the
new man

"...put on the new man who is renewed in knowledge according to the image of Him who created him" (Colossians 3:10, NKJ).

We now come to the fourth and last step in entering into our new spiritual dimension. This step is what Paul calls, "putting on the new man."

In the book of Ephesians he tells us: *"Strip yourselves of your former nature—put off and discard your old unrenewed self...And be constantly renewed in the spirit of your mind—having a fresh mental and spiritual attitude; and **put on the new nature**...created in God's image (Godlike) in true righteousness and holiness" (Ephesians 4:22-24, TAB).*

Exactly what do we mean by putting on the "new man" or "new nature"...and how do we go about doing it?

In essence, what "putting on the new man" amounts to is putting on new attitudes.

What attitudes are we to put on?

We are to put on the new attitudes of an overcomer!

Just what is an "attitude"? It is a mental position (or stand) that we assume for a specific purpose. Therefore, most of our behavior is dictated by our attitudes.

For example, if we assume a negative attitude, we are going to react negatively when we feel threatened, or someone challenges us.

If we have a fearful attitude, we will react in fear.

If we have a critical attitude, we will react to circumstances in our own self-interest and self-defense.

Every attitude that could possibly exist in any of our lives falls into one of two categories: It is either an attitude leading to life, or one which leads to death. There is nothing in between.

All the attitudes of our old nature ultimately contribute to death. These include attitudes of unforgiveness, doubt, unbelief, fear, hostility, hatred, anger and so forth.

The problem is that we often do not recognize the fact that our old attitudes are harmful to the renewed life of our minds in Him. Thus, we continue to serve the Lord without being cleansed of them, not realizing that they place barriers between us and the answers to our prayers.

How easy it is to fall into the trap described in the book of Proverbs which says, *"There is a way which seems right to a man, but its end is the way of death" (Proverbs 14:12, NKJ).*

The attitudes of our new man (under the dominion of the Holy Spirit) are attitudes of life. These include attitudes of praise, thanksgiving, faith, hope, love, mercy, compassion, and all the other attitudes seen in our Lord.

The challenge each one of us faces every day is to be willing to die to all our attitudes of death (the old nature) and replace them with attitudes of life...which are the attitudes of the overcomer!

This entire process of becoming a triumphant overcomer in Christ is a major part of God's will for you.

In fact, being an overcomer is so important to Him that eight times in the book of Revelation, He states it as the criterion for inheriting the rewards of His Kingdom. God summarizes the significance He places on overcoming by promising us: *"He that overcometh shall inherit all things" (Revelation 21:7).*

Why is overcoming so important to God? Because by

overcoming, what we are actually doing is destroying the works of the devil, and that is expressly what He sent His Son to this earth to do.

Jesus told us that His meat was to do the will of the Father *(John 4:34)*. And the Father's will for Him was dramatically expressed in one powerful sentence related by the Apostle John: *"...For this purpose the Son of God was manifested, that He might destroy the works of the devil" (1 John 3:8, NKJ)*.

Yes, the very reason that God sent His Son to this earth was to do His will by overcoming death with Life!

As the sons of God through Jesus Christ, we are called by God to do the same thing!

This can only be accomplished when we put on an attitude of offensive warfare against the enemy.

Satan and his army of demonic forces are forever plotting to destroy God's holy ones. They are constantly sending out Satan's "little foxes" to subtly, yet ferociously, destroy the fruit of the Spirit.

Unless we learn to stand firm with our minds completely surrendered to the Holy Spirit, and protected by the overcoming attitudes of the new man, we will give Satan a foothold, and through our own negativity, crumble to the temptations of our old natures.

Jesus told us: *"The thief cometh not, but for to steal, to kill, and to destroy: I am come that they might have life, and that they might have it more abundantly" (John 10:10)*.

Are we ready for His abundant life to flow through us by rising up to overcome all forces that would destroy us...and others?

I hope you are ready, because *"The night is far spent, the day is at hand. Therefore let us cast off the works of darkness, and let us put on the armor of light" (Romans 13:12, NKJ)*.

Put on a new attitude

As we prepare to actively become the victors that God wants us to be, we discover that there are two phases to putting on the attitudes of an overcomer.

The first is to know and believe that your new nature is dead to all sin, and what you are dead to, you are totally free from reacting to in any way!

This doesn't mean that your old nature won't flare up and give you trouble. Paul testifies that the old nature of the flesh wages war against the Spirit and the Spirit against the flesh constantly *(Galatians 5:17)*. But by seeing yourself as dead to the urgings of the flesh, they will have no dominion over you. Paul explicitly tells us: *"...consider yourselves also dead to sin and your relation to it broken, but (that you are) alive to God—living in unbroken fellowship with Him—in Christ Jesus...For sin shall not (any longer) exert dominion over you, since now you are not under Law (as slaves), but under grace..." (Romans 6:11,14, TAB).*

From these passages we can see that the second phase in putting on our new attitudes is to see ourselves alive to Christ...and His life within us! To know...believe...and see that: *"I am crucified with Christ: nevertheless I live; yet not I, but Christ liveth in me: and the life which I now live in the flesh I live by the faith of the Son of God, who loved me, and gave himself for me" (Galatians 2:20).*

What tremendous work of restoration God is doing in each of us through teaching us to overcome all darkness with His life! *"For if while we were enemies we were reconciled to God through the death of His Son, it is much more (certain), now that we are reconciled, that we shall be saved (daily delivered from sin's dominion) through His (resurrection) life" (Romans 5:10, TAB).*

Let's now look at how to apply our new attitudes to our lives. To do this, once again we look at the life of Paul to "find ourselves" in God's Word through the example that Paul sets.

In II Corinthians, Chapter Twelve, we see that Paul had an infirmity (or weakness) that Satan continuously took advantage of to try to pound him into defeat. Paul called this problem his "thorn."

His first course of action was the one most of us would take: he appealed to the Lord three times to remove it (verse 8).

In this stage of his life, it was the Lord's will that Paul overcome it through the new resurrection life within him.

Christ told him, *"My grace (unmerited assistance) is sufficient for thee: for my strength is made perfect in weakness" (II Corinthians 12:9).*

At this point, Paul had a choice of "putting on" one of

two attitudes. He could either murmur, fight against God's will and give in to the weakness of the old nature, giving a foothold to Satan, or he could put on an attitude of an overcomer.

Which course did he take? He chose God's way by saying: *"...Therefore, I will all the more gladly glory in my weaknesses and infirmities, that the strength and power of Christ, the Messiah, may rest...upon me! So for the sake of Christ, I am well pleased and take pleasure in infirmities, insults, hardships, persecutions, perplexities and distresses; for when I am weak (in human strength), then am I (truly) strong — able, powerful in divine strength" (II Corinthians 12:9-10, TAB).*

Paul knew that although adversity might come against him, it had no power over him as long as he chose to exercise the life of Christ within him.

Choose the path of victory!

Stop for a moment and take inventory in your life. What attitudes of darkness or defeat hidden in your mind can you exchange today for new attitudes of being an overcomer?

Are you secretly depressed...mentally or spiritually? Are you confused or discouraged? Do you feel like you have been lost in a "spiritual desert" for some time and are wondering if the Lord has forgotten you?

Do you remember how you sang and rejoiced in the Lord when you were first saved and wonder if those days are gone forever?

If so, let's use your situation as an example to see how we can apply the four steps we have been discussing to bring you into a new understanding of your condition. As we do, you will see that God has allowed this period of "dryness" in your life for a purpose. You will realize it is now His will for you to use this experience for His glory!

First, find yourself in His Word. Where in the Bible is there an example of a person (or people) in a "wilderness" walk with God?

The book of Hosea shows us just such a description of what you have been going through...from the Lord's perspective. In Chapter Two, He says: *"Therefore, behold, I will allure her (Israel) and bring her into the wilderness, and I will speak tenderly and to her heart. There I will give her her*

*vineyards, and make the Valley of Achor or Troubling to
be for her a door of hope and expectation. And she shall
sing there and respond as in the days of her youth, and as
at the time when she came up out of the land of Egypt"
(Hosea 2:14-15, TAB).*

As astounding as this may sound, the Lord is actually telling
us here that it is He Who brings us into these wilderness
experiences so that He may speak tenderly to us (get our
attention), and that it is in these "valleys of troubling" that
He will open to us doors of hope and expectation. It is here
that we will learn to sing to Him again!

Hope and expectation are attitudes. They are attitudes of
life; attitudes of the overcomer. When the Lord brings us
through the valleys, we have the choice of taking either the
path of victory or the path of defeat...depending on our
attitudes.

We can choose to wallow in self-pity, anger, or confusion;
or, we can see ourselves as steadfastly faithful to Him,
surrender all negative feelings, and use the time to think of
ways we can give to Him! Sing to Him! And then, in hope
and expectancy, wait for the revelations and new intimacy
He longs so much to impart.

You are being prepared as the bride of our Lord. Are you
willing to see yourself robed in all the attitudes that bring
Him pleasure?

Are you willing to surrender any aspects of your nature
that would block this...and make pleasing Him your first
priority...no matter what outward conditions may exist?

Last, are you willing to put on the new attitudes of the
overcomer, and through the power of His life within you,
die to all the old habits and thoughts that would hinder
complete faith in His Word?

Right now, God is calling you to: *"Arise, from the
depression and prostration in which circumstances have
kept you; rise to a new life! Shine—be radiant with the glory
of the Lord; for your light is come, and the glory of the Lord
is risen upon you!" (Isaiah 60:1, TAB).*

The battle tactics of the new man

Around 500 B.C., a Chinese military genius by the name
of Sun Tzu wrote a little book called *The Art of War*. Although
it is now nearly 2,500 years old, this collection of Sun Tzu's

insights are still required reading in almost every military academy in the world, and many modern military strategists have closely followed his instructions for waging a successful war.

All truth is parallel, and some of Sun Tzu's thoughts are as applicable to spiritual warfare as they are to warfare in the world. One of the principles Sun Tzu maintained was if you don't know your enemy, and you don't know yourself, you are almost sure to lose any battle. If you do know yourself, but don't know your enemy, you have half a chance of winning. But if you know yourself and you know your enemy, you are sure to win!

What has this to do with us? Everything. Many of you may still be frustrated in your attempt to put on your new man because you don't know your enemy. You are in the midst of a vicious invisible war over your soul, and the powers of darkness aren't sleeping. We cannot sleep either. So, let us proceed to several guidelines for waging a successful spiritual battle.

STRATEGY 1
Know the enemies in your life

We all have our "weak spots"...areas in our lives where we are particularly vulnerable to enemy attacks. It is these areas which Satan will consistently try to use to weaken our whole spiritual structure. However, until you specifically identify these enemies in your life, you are in no position to overcome them.

All enemies have names; names such as fear, bitterness, unforgiveness, hatred, resentment, competitiveness, lust, doubt or greed. These are the same names as the negative attitudes of the old man, because it is these foul spirits which help to fuel these attitudes in our lives and keep them "stirred up."

Sooner or later all enemies that hinder your life in the Spirit must be dealt with, whether they are your own attitudes or Satan's forces. You can identify the root cause of many attacks immediately, but there are some that can only be exposed by the Holy Spirit in periods of waiting on the Lord.

In fact, the deeper you go in your relationship with the Lord, the more you will have to depend on Him to expose the root causes of many attitude problems that are beyond your natural ability to recognize.

Once the Lord has revealed a problem area in your life, hold it up to Him to be cleansed and refilled with His power. He promises that: *"If we confess our sins, He is faithful and just to forgive our sins and to cleanse us from all unrighteousness" (I John 1:9, NKJ).*

If He gives you the discernment to see that some foul spirit is contributing to your behavior, rebuke it in the Name of Jesus. Tell the devil to get on his side of the line! Stand firm in the Word of God.

However, once this has taken place, always be on guard for your own weakness in this area (with the expectation of attaining complete victory). Satan doesn't give up lost territory easily, and he is very likely to try to hinder your life again in the same spot!

Therefore, our next strategy point is absolutely essential.

STRATEGY 2
Know how the enemy operates

In the long run, knowing how the enemy works is just as valuable as recognizing who he is. For instance, you may clearly see that you are often plagued by attacks of fear. But when are these assaults most likely to come? What is Satan's strategy?

Does he most likely "hit" when you are tired? Or right after you have moved out in faith for the Lord?

How does he launch his attack? Is it through the criticism of your friends? Or through the discouragement of your family?

When you study when and how these assaults come on your life, you will soon see a pattern. As Paul puts it: *"...we are not ignorant of his (Satan's) devices" (II Corinthians 2:11).*

Once you see a pattern, you can be all ready with an offensive strategy which will firmly squelch all his power over your life.

STRATEGY 3
Have an offensive plan ready

In an army battle, plans are made up long before the soldiers march out onto the field.

Now that you know who the enemy is, what weaknesses

he is most likely to take advantage of...and the tactics he is most likely to use...be ready!

Be ready to change your behavior in that situation based on the new image of yourself as a child of God. See yourself acting and responding as His chosen one would act.

Be ready to immediately surrender your will to God in any troubling situation. Have your battle plan set in your mind and heart. Know how you are going to react when adversity arises. Keep your eye firmly set on God's Word and His power within you to guide you anytime...anywhere.

As the writer of Proverbs instructs us: *"My son, attend to my words; consent and submit to my sayings. Let them not depart from your sight; keep them in the center of your heart...Keep your heart with all vigilance and above all that you guard, for out of it flow the springs of life"* (Proverbs 4:20-21,23, TAB).

With your new image of yourself as God's soldier now firmly implanted, let's look at our fourth strategy point.

STRATEGY 4
Be equipped to resist attack

Your "equipment" for any kind of spiritual battle consists of four things:

1. The power of Christ's love within you
2. Your new attitude of being an overcomer
3. The Word of God itself...the *"sword of the Spirit"...which is your major offensive weapon against any onslaught* (Ephesians 6:17).
4. Constant prayer. By "prayer" we mean all types of communion with God ranging from worship, to waiting on Him, to fervent intercession. The object of this is that any mind strongly planted in the throne room of God through continual prayer (in whatever form it takes) is not going to open itself to the enemy's devices.

Now let's go on to the final—and most crucial—aspect of putting on our new man...the attitude which, when applied to your life, will dynamically loose God's guidance for you!

Chapter 8

The commandment that looses God's guidance

"He who says he is in the light, and hates his brother, is in darkness until now. He who loves his brother abides in the light, and there is no cause for stumbling in him" (I John 2:9-10, NKJ).

As we learn to put on our new inner man, there is one more attitude that is so important to God that He devotes an entire chapter of His Word to reveal it to us.

What is that attitude? It is the attitude that we have toward each other!

As startling as it may sound, receiving God's guidance on our part is directly dependent upon our willingness to surrender...not only to God but to each other!

In addition, God has ordained that submitting to one another in love is a prerequisite to receiving not only guidance from Him, but revelation as well.

You say, "Brother Cerullo, I never heard that before." You haven't? Well, the children of Israel certainly did, because the 58th chapter of the book of Isaiah is devoted to it.

In this chapter, we see that the people of Israel were crying out for God's guidance just as much as Christians are today. The Lord says: *"...day after day they seek me out; they seem eager to know my ways...They ask me for just decisions and seem eager for God to come near them" (Isaiah 58:2, NIV).*

Isaiah then tells how his people thought that they would receive God's guidance if they fasted. Thus, the Jews became very conscientious about this ritual. They not only fasted, but went through great theatrics along with it.

They mourned and tore their clothes. The Amplified Bible says they even *"afflicted themselves."* Somehow it didn't seem to do any good. The more they carried on, the less He seemed to hear.

"Don't You see us?" they cried to the Lord. "Hey, we're putting on a great show for You down here. Why aren't You answering us?"

Isn't this what we do today? We fast; we go to services and wail before the Lord...but inside our hearts, nothing is changed. God wasn't any more impressed with this approach to receiving guidance in Isaiah's day than He is now.

He quickly pointed out to them: *"...on the day of your fasting, you do as you please and exploit all your workers. Your fasting ends in quarreling and strife, and in striking each other with wicked fists. You cannot fast as you do today and expect your voice to be heard on high" (Isaiah 58:3-4, NIV).*

This is a fairly strong reproach, yet when we skip down to verse 11 we suddenly see the Lord telling this same group: *"The LORD will guide you always; he will satisfy your needs in a sun-scorched land and will strengthen your frame. You will be like a well-watered garden, like a spring whose waters never fail" (Isaiah 58:11, NIV).*

Now, what in the world accounted for this incredible change in the Lord's tone? Why was He suddenly promising them guidance and strength? What went on between verses four and eleven?

What happened was that the Lord laid down conditions which His people must fulfill with each other if He were to lead them through!

He was telling them in no uncertain terms that a breakthrough in the way they treated each other was absolutely necessary if they expected to receive further revelation of Him and His will.

Therefore, let's examine just what He told them to do (and not to do) if they wanted His guidance.

First, He told them: *"Is not this the kind of fasting I have chosen: to loose the chains of injustice and untie the cords of the yoke, to set the oppressed free and break every yoke? Is it not to share your food with the hungry and to provide the poor wanderer with shelter—when you see the naked, to clothe him, and not to turn away from your own flesh and blood? Then your light will break forth like the dawn, and your healing will quickly appear; then your righteousness will go before you, and the glory of the LORD will be your rear guard. Then you will call, and the LORD will answer; you will cry for help, and he will say: Here am I"* (Isaiah 58:6-9, NIV).

Remember as you read this that all truth is parallel. Just as there are various types of physical oppression and physical yokes of bondage, so there are also numerous forms of mental and spiritual oppressions that we impose on one another. How do we do this? Through attitudes of unforgiveness, division, strife, anger, bitterness, resentment, and all the other negative thoughts that we shoot like arrows into each other's souls.

These are the types of yokes that are being applied on every member of the Body of Christ today by our own spiritual attitudes. These are the bondages the Lord wants done away with now if we are to come into full communion with Him!

Let's read on. The next thing the Lord tells His people is: *"...if you do away with the yoke of oppression, with the pointing finger and malicious talk, and if you spend yourselves on behalf of the hungry and satisfy the needs of the oppressed, then your light will rise in the darkness, and your night will become like the noonday. The LORD will guide you always..."* (Isaiah 58:9-11, NIV).

Are we ready, as the children of God, to surrender all our cherished attitudes of "individuality" which we have so fiercely protected, to give ourselves sacrificially to one another?

I prophesy to you that very soon God is going to have a people who *practice what they preach.* What each one of us will have to decide is: "Do we want to be obedient to His will by dying to ourselves; or do we want to step out of His will, do our own thing, and ultimately be cast into outer darkness like the five ladies who didn't make it into the marriage feast? (Matthew 25:1-13).

For years the Church of Jesus Christ has been one of the major organizations on earth that kills its wounded. Now God is saying, "that's enough!"

To illustrate the tragic, long-reaching effects of what we have been doing to each other, let me share with you an experience I had while I was in England conducting a crusade.

One afternoon I passed through the hotel lobby in Manchester, England, where a business machine convention was being conducted. Since I'm interested in computers, I asked if I could go in, and the official said, "Certainly. Go on through."

As I was looking at the consoles, I was suddenly drawn in my spirit to walk up to a certain man and talk with him. We started chatting, and I felt led by the Holy Spirit to say, "Sir, what did you used to do before you were an executive in this computer company?"

He was quite startled, and answered, "Why do you ask me that?"

I said, "Never mind. Would you mind sharing it with me?"

He got red in the face and told me, "I was a preacher."

I replied, "Isn't that strange? I'm a preacher. What denomination were you?"

He became even redder and said, "I was Pentecostal."

This made me quite curious, so I pressed him some more. "Would you mind telling me why you left the ministry?"

Big tears came to his eyes as he said, "No. I don't mind telling you. I'm not a Christian. I'm an atheist. For years I went around preaching. But all I could see was this terrible hypocrisy among the preachers. I couldn't stand it. I thought, 'If this is the ministry, I don't want anything to do with it.' I looked at Christians' lives and said, 'If this is the way Christians live who claim to have so much of God, I won't have anything to do with it!' "

Hearing this, I reached out, took him by the hand and put my arm around him. I told him how much I loved him, and that I was going right up to my room and pray for him.

Now we all know Christians are not perfect and most of all we are not supposed to put our eyes on man...period! Christ is our Example.

The horrifying reality is that this man is not an isolated

case. Millions of people see what goes on between so-called Christians and react just like he did. However, all this is changing. In our day. God is going to have a people who are so united in love with one another that no power on earth will stop them from manifesting the very Presence of Jesus Christ to the world!

Do you know the biggest reason why so far we have had very few deep relationships with one another? Because we are not keeping God's commandments. We have refused to see ourselves as a people who walk in obedience to His every word. You see, it's easy to walk in His love and His perfect will when you are walking in obedience. When you are doing your own thing, it's impossible.

Shortly before He died, our Lord issued a new commandment to all those who would be His true disciples throughout the ages. He said: *"A new commandment I give to you, that you love one another. By this all will know that you are My disciples, if you have love for one another"* (John 13:34-35, NKJ).

There is a whole world of starving, spiritually emaciated people out there who are waiting to see the same love that the Father has for the Son, and that the Son has for the Church, demonstrated in us!

Those in the world have never experienced true love, and they don't have real relationships. At best, they are weak and frail and phony.

They are looking at us, but so far they have seen very little relationship between Christians. Why? Because we have not been willing to die to ourselves enough to form the kinds of relationships that will give us the strength to care! The strength to overcome! The strength to reach the world!

Jesus said: *"Most assuredly, I say to you, unless a grain of wheat falls into the ground and dies, it remains alone..."* (John 12:24, NKJ).

Our problem has been that we've been willing to remain alone. We have not taken the time for each other's needs.

Can I ask you a question? How long has it been since you felt the pain, or helped carry the torments of a brother in distress?

Perhaps you don't care to answer this. But God, by the power of His Holy Spirit in your renewed mind, is about to make His love for your brothers come so alive in you that your entire attitude toward people will be revolutionized.

Through the restoration of your inner man, the day will come when you will sit in Pennsylvania and (in the Spirit) feel the infirmities of someone in California.

You won't have to read in the newspapers about persecution in Central America. You will feel it in your prayer closet, and fervently intercede to rescue your brothers from defeat.

When this begins to take place, an amazing thing will start to happen. As you are forced to "crowd closer" to the Lord for guidance and strength for your brothers, you will be drawn into greater intimacy with Him than you ever dreamed possible.

The more you cling to Him and draw deeply from His rich resources within you, the more He will pour revelation and guidance into your spirit!

Paul dramatically described this process when he said: *"(For my concern is) that their hearts may be braced (comforted, cheered and encouraged) as they are knit together in love...that they may become progressively more intimately acquainted with, and may know more definitely...that mystic secret of God (which is) Christ, the Anointed One"* (Colossians 2:2, TAB).

The miracle of all this is that you don't have to do a thing in your own strength. It's all the strength of God in your new inner man doing the work.

That is why Jesus could require us to follow His "new commandment"...because we are not the ones to carry it out. Our job is merely to surrender to His perfect will...and let Him do the rest. It's the power of His Holy Spirit within us that will nurture and manifest His love for others through us to such an extent that eventually even our foes will be reconciled to Him!

We're made rich by each other!

Throughout this book we have been concentrating on how each of us individually can come into greater fellowship with God, and as a result, know His will for our lives.

Now, let's apply the same steps we've learned to actively break down the barriers with each other!

First, find and see yourself in the Word of God. Thus far you have focused on building a new inner vision of yourself as a child of God. Now, ask the Holy Spirit to guide you to portions of God's Word that will help you build a new vision of your relationship with someone with whom you have been having problems.

Be willing to let Him show you a new perspective of what that individual may have suffered in his life...and what rich potential is hidden in his new nature, now. Begin to visualize that person in a new light. Most importantly, start to see yourself as reacting differently when you are together.

Throughout this exercise, first see yourself as the minister of reconciliation that God created you to be, not only to reconcile lost souls to Him, but your weaker brother as well. For God *"gave to us the ministry of reconciliation—that by word and deed we might aim to bring others into harmony with Him" (II Corinthians 5:18, TAB).*

Secondly, surrender your will concerning this relationship, to God. If you are carrying any negative attitudes toward this person, hand them over to Him. Allow His Spirit to replace old, destructive thoughts with new ones of life, love and reconciliation.

Thirdly, make the love of God your number one priority in this relationship. This may be extremely difficult when you are dealing with rebellious, hostile, or manipulative people, but as the Lord says: *"...if you love those who love you, what credit is that to you? For even sinners love those who love them" (Luke 6:32, NKJ).*

Fourthly, put on a new attitude toward this person; an attitude of meekness, gentleness, humility and compassion. *"Let this same attitude and purpose and (humble) mind be in you which was in Christ Jesus—Let Him be your example in humility..." (Philippians 2:5, TAB).*

As you take these steps, the Holy Spirit will soften your heart and renew your mind toward this person. For I pray that God *"may grant you a spirit of wisdom and revelation...so that you can know and understand the hope to which He has called you and how rich is His glorious inheritance in the saints—His set apart ones" (Ephesians 1:17-18, TAB).*

The full apppreciation of the valuable inheritance that He has in each of us is one of the richest purposes of revelation!

Our Lord's greatest desire

No man ever had such a deep, penetrating love for mankind as Jesus did. His was a love that overcame the world. It was a love that caused him to weep over Jerusalem, even though He was rejected. It was a love that longed to reach out; to touch, and to unify.

Therefore, in His last time of prayer with His disciples, just before He was beaten, tortured and crucified, Jesus won, through intercession, a breakthrough in the spirit world that would solidify and unify His Church forever.

That last night, He passionately petitioned the Father: *"I pray...that all of them may be one, Father, just as you are in me and I am in you. May they also be in us so that the world may believe that you have sent me. I have given them the glory that you gave me, that they may be one as we are one: I in them and you in me. May they be brought to complete unity to let the world know that you sent me and have loved them even as you have loved me"* (John 17:20-23, NIV).

Right now, before our very eyes, this prayer is being fulfilled in His endtime Church. It is almost overwhelming to think that through His love to us, many in the world will see Him; believe in Him, and accept Him now!

Take a moment to pray with me this prayer of agreement and thanksgiving for all He is doing in your life to fulfill His will that we all be one!

Heavenly Father, You are going to have a people, a people who walk in harmony with Your perfect will. We thank and praise You that You are breaking every band of selfishness in each of us; You are breaking every chain of our self-centeredness; You are helping us to take our eyes off ourselves, and giving us the ability to die to our old natures.

Father, You are bringing forth that ultimate intention of Yours...the restoration of Your life in us, and ours in You, binding and knitting our hearts together in the power of Your love.

You are making us closer to each other than we are to our own flesh and blood. Through Your mighty work of restoration in each of our lives, You are bringing us together in a new family...one that is one with You, Your Son and Your Holy Spirit. We praise You for bringing us into this new spiritual dimension of unity and love.

It is here, as we walk with You that Your will for our lives will be manifested in us. Never again will we struggle to know Your will. As You were, so are we in this world. We are Your will and through us Your will is extended into this world.

Chapter 9

Let love be your guide

...when He, the Spirit of truth, has come, He will guide you into all truth; for He will not speak on His own authority, but whatever He hears He will speak; and He will tell you things to come" (John 16:13, NKJ).

Although we have explored many guidelines as to how to come into greater communion with God (resulting in knowing God's will for our lives), there will be times when you cannot seem to experience Him at all; times when you feel totally out of touch with Him; times when He seems to have withdrawn from you.

It is during these periods when you may begin to wonder:

"What do I do if I cannot seem to hear from God when I am pressed to make a decision?"

"What do I do if I have been deceived, acted on what I thought was God's voice...but wasn't?"

"How do I know if the failures in my ministry were in God's will or not?"

"Is it possible that I have fallen so far away from God that I cannot find the way back?"

In each of these instances there are two important truths which will comfort and guide you no matter what you go through.

The first is that His love is always guiding you, whether you experience it or not. Even Jesus was led into a "wilderness" experience, as part of God's will for Him. Be assured that even if you willfully take a wrong turn, His love is always there trying to guide you out of it.

The second guideline is whenever you have doubts as to what to do, let love be your guide. Whenever there is a decision you must make, and you have not received any clearcut direction from Him or His Word, stop and ask yourself, **"What would love do?"**

Let's examine these two guidelines, and how they apply to your life.

His love is always guiding you

There are several promises that God makes to us in His Word that sometimes seem quite hard for us to believe, promises such as: *"Never will I leave you; never will I forsake you" (Hebrews 13:5, NIV). "...I will lead them in paths they have not known. I will make darkness light before them, and crooked places straight. These things I will do for them, and not forsake them" (Isaiah 42:16, NKJ).*

These passages may seem especially difficult to comprehend if we have recently been deceived by the enemy or made a wrong move.

The Word of God has several examples where God's people were deceived or tricked. Yet, God always had His chosen ones right in the palm of His hand. Miraculously, through the power of His love and mercy, He turned what could have been tragic situations around for His glory.

One example is the story of Isaac. In the 27th chapter of Genesis (verses 18-29) we see that Isaac was deceived into bestowing his blessing on the wrong son. With Rebekah's help, Jacob had dressed up as Esau to trick his aging father into giving him the blessing of the firstborn, instead of his brother.

Although Isaac was wary that Jacob's voice did not sound like Esau's, nonetheless, he fell for the ploy.

Now, if this had happened to any of us, we probably would have looked at this deception within the framework of our own limited minds and thought, "Oh, God! I've been deceived. Look what I've done! It's all over now!"

But our Father is bigger than all this. He knew from the foundation of the earth that such mistakes, errors in judgment, or hasty actions would be made—all as a part of growing up...and He provided for them.

In His rich mercy incomprehensible, He saw our stumbling blocks long before we did, and made plans for them to become stepping stones.

God knew before the foundation of the earth that Isaac would be deceived, and He provided for it. He incorporated it into His plan, which is far more vast, far greater than any of our errors.

So what about what looks to us as periods of failure in our lives or ministries?

Our Lord encountered the same feeling you go through when (to the natural eye) His healing ministry failed dismally in His own hometown (Mark 6:5-6). However, His attitude of unwavering trust and confidence in His Father's love overcame any doubts, fear, or frustration that could ever arise from that situation.

If there is one thing that penetrates your spirit now, let it be this: Believe with your whole heart, mind, soul, and spirit in God's love for you!

Know that He is always with you and watching over you.

Be willing to see yourself in the life of David, who, despite ferocious persecution and torment at the hands of Saul, still trusted and rejoiced in God, saying: *"Where could I go from Your Spirit? Or where could I flee from Your presence? If I ascend up into Heaven, You are there; if I make my bed in Sheol (the place of the dead), behold, You are there. If I take the wings of the morning and dwell in the uttermost parts of the sea, Even there shall Your hand lead me, and Your right hand shall hold me" (Psalm 139:7-10, TAB).*

A word to backsliders

Occasionally a partner will come to me in deep distress and say, "Brother Cerullo, you don't know what I have done. I'm afraid I have fallen so far away from the Lord that He won't take me back again. But I want so desperately to come back. What can I do?"

Please, if any of you have been brutally tricked by Satan

into thinking that God does not want you back, recognize it right now as the lie that it is! God wants you back at all costs. Jesus' parable about going after the one lost sheep was for you *(Luke 15:4-7)*. The parable about the woman rejoicing over the one lost coin was for you *(Luke 15:8-10)*.

The sixth chapter of the book of Hebrews is also for you. It is possible to fall beyond repentance, **but,** to do so you must consciously have experienced several things. The Word specifically tells us that *"it is impossible to restore and bring again to repentance those who..."*

1. Were *"once for all enlightened, who have consciously tasted the heavenly gift, and have become sharers of the Holy Spirit" (verse 4, TAB)*.

2. *"And have felt how good the Word of God is and the mighty powers of the age and world to come" (verse 5, TAB)*.

Then and only then, if they *"deviate from the faith and turn away from their allegiance"*...purposely trample on the blood of Jesus and mock the work of the Holy Spirit...are they in serious trouble.

In my 39 years of ministry I do not recall one person who ever fulfilled both these conditions and then turned their back on God.

Quite the contrary, most of the Church today is so blinded, and so confused, that very few people have fully experienced even two of these areas, much less all of them. Most Christians are a far cry from having *"felt the mighty powers of the age and world to come."* They are yearning just to recognize the voice of God in their hearts.

If you are one of those who is chained in cords of condemnation concerning what you may or may not have done to God in the past, be delivered from your guilt! Know that Jesus is telling you the same thing He told the woman who was caught in adultery: *"neither do I condemn you; go and sin no more" (John 8:11, NKJ)*.

Believe the intensity of His love and His faithfulness toward you. Right now, in deep concern, He is holding His nail-scarred hands out to you, saying: *" 'I know the plans I have for you,' declares the LORD, 'plans to prosper you and not to harm you, plans to give you hope and a future. Then you will call upon me and come and pray to me, and I will listen to you. You will seek me and find me when you seek me with all your heart. I will be found by you,' declares the LORD" (Jeremiah 29:11-14, NIV).*

Let love be your guide

As you begin to experience the revelation power of God flowing from your innermost being, and learn to know and discern His will, you will see more miraculous answers to prayer than you have ever had in your entire life.

You will come to know that you know, that you know, that God has planted a **new seed** deep within your spiritual and physical being.

It is a seed of revelation; it is a seed of love; it is a seed of faith; and it is a seed of power, and it will grow and bear fruit until Jesus comes.

How many of you know that when you first conceive a child...just a little seed...nothing is formed? But steadily it grows, and grows, and grows, until finally birth takes place.

That full birth will finally come when you and I are changed in the twinkling of an eye at our Lord's return. Then, the full manifestation of what you are intended to be, through the work of God in Christ in you, will be completed in a split second of time.

Meanwhile, that precious seed of Christ's nature within you is being formed and I, like the Apostle Paul, travail in prayer for each of you until it comes to maturity in your life. As Paul said: *"My little children, for whom I labor in birth again until Christ is formed in you" (Galatians 4:19, NKJ).*

You will find that as His love comes to fruition in you, and you are brought into deeper communion with it, that it will guide you in all your steps...in all your decisions, all your trials and turns.

But believe me, being guided into complete harmony with His will in your outer circumstances is only one phase of your new journey into intimacy with God. There is so much more that God has in store for you that we haven't even scratched the surface. God Himself says: *" 'Eye has not seen, nor ear heard, nor have entered into the heart of man the things which God has prepared for those who love Him.' But God has revealed them to us through His Spirit" (I Corinthians 2:9-10, NKJ).*

His Word also says: *"...He lavished upon us...every kind of wisdom and understanding..." (Ephesians 1:8, TAB).*

Yes, like the father of the prodigal son, God is looking at

His children being restored to Him in the power of communion with Him, and He is saying, "My son was dead and now he is alive!"

How I praise God that you and I live in the most exciting generation of the ages; the generation in which we are each being granted an outpouring of His Spirit of wisdom and revelation into the mysteries and deep knowledge of Him.

What a privilege and responsibility it is to know that there is not one of us who has to grope in the dark, wondering where He is. For it is His express purpose that each one of us come to know God's will for our lives...and He has graciously lavished on us everything we need to do it!

Chapter 10

Destroy
Satan's lies

"...For this purpose the Son of God was manifested, that He might destroy the works of the devil" (I John 3:8, NKJ).

I n spite of all the promises of God's Word...in spite of all the revelation knowledge available to the Church today...in spite of the great outpouring of God's Holy Spirit, countless Christians are still suffering defeat and falling short of God's perfect will.

Why? Because Satan and his demonic forces have tricked them into being double-minded concerning God's Word. Satan has swindled them through his lies!

Due to the enemy's deceptions, many people have fallen into a state where (with half their minds) they believe that every promise in God's Word is His will...and, (with the other half of their minds) they listen to the enemy!

The devil tells them things like: "These promises aren't for everyone. You're an exception." Or, "God doesn't work miracles for His children today. He only did that for the early Church."

I cannot tell you how it grieves me to see God's people

fail to appropriate all that God is holding out to them because Satan has convinced them that our Father's provisions are only for a select few!

Therefore, I want to help you break through all the confusion and see exactly what God's will is in the areas of greatest concern to Christians today.

These areas are:

1. **Health**
2. **Prosperity**
3. **Family unity**
4. **Unsaved loved ones**
5. **Ministry opportunities**

Let's "take the mask off" and open our eyes to God's highest will for our lives.

God's perfect will for your health

"Beloved, I wish above all things that thou mayest prosper and be in health, even as thy soul prospereth" (III John 2).

In the Word of God there are many scriptures which confirm without a doubt that one of the purposes that God sent His Son to die on the cross, was to destroy all the works of the devil concerning sickness and disease. The prophet Isaiah reveals, *"...He was wounded for our transgressions, He was bruised for our iniquities; The chastisement for our peace was upon Him, And by His stripes we are healed"* *(Isaiah 53:5, NKJ)*.

The Psalmist David confirms, *"He sent His word and healed them, And delivered them from their destructions"* *(Psalm 107:20, NKJ)*.

In addition, the New Testament emphatically describes how, *"...Jesus went about all the cities and villages...healing every sickness and every disease among the people"* *(Matthew 9:35, NKJ)*.

However, as soon as many of us accept the seeds of healing given to us in God's Word, we are attacked with doubts. For we also see in the Bible that Paul recommended a little wine for Timothy's stomach problem *(I Timothy 5:23);* that another brother named Epaphroditus *"was sick almost unto death"* (Philippians 2:25-27, NKJ); and that Paul had to leave another co-worker behind because this man was so ill *(II Timothy 4:20)*.

In the book of I Corinthians we are even told that Paul

turned one member of the congregation over to Satan: *"for the destruction of the flesh, that his spirit may be saved...(I Corinthians 5:5, NKJ)*. (This was the man who had engaged in an illicit relationship with his father's wife, but whom the Corinthian church had neglected to discipline.)

After reading these things, turmoil sometimes sets in concerning God's will. It is then that people say to me, "Brother Cerullo, I'm confused. I thought God's promises applied to everyone. How do I know that His promises are for me? Is sickness sometimes a part of suffering for His sake?"

Thus, we can see that people often become snared by what they think are contradictions in God's Word. This is a problem which we will encounter as we explore all five areas of God's will (health, prosperity, family unity, unsaved loved ones, and ministry opportunities).

If we look hard enough, we can always find what seem to be exceptions to God's perfect will scattered throughout the Bible. Whenever we find these passages we are faced with a choice: We can either focus our attention on the exceptions to God's perfect will (such as the fact that God permits sickness), or use as our **goal** (as our **ideal**) His perfect will itself...which is health.

However, we must note that when we honestly examine what seem to be the exceptions to God's will in the Bible, we discover that in most cases someone fell short of God's perfect will; so our Father, in His infinite mercy, made special provisions for that person!

One example of this is the individual whom Paul turned over to Satan *(I Corinthians 5:5)*. Now, ask yourself, "What was God's perfect will for this man?"

First and foremost, God's will was for that son to be restored back to Him...body, mind, soul and spirit. Then, in the process of being reconciled back to Him, it was God's will that he come into the perfect health that Jesus paid for on the cross.

But what happened? Instead of accepting all that God offered him through the path of obedience, he chose the path of rebellion and sexual sin. Therefore, God allowed the destruction of the flesh so that in the end the most important part of that man (his spirit) might be saved!

Did God's **perfect will** for the man ever change? No.

Was His will any different for this backslidden man than for anyone else in the congregation? No.

Did Jesus pay any less a price for this person than He did for any of us who are in excellent health? No.

But for every promise in the Bible there is a condition or prerequisite that we must do before God can fulfill His promise to us.

When we are obedient to the conditions that God lays down, and show it through taking positive steps of faith, God will give us all we need to bring glory to Him in all the areas of our lives.

For example, let's look at Psalm 91 (NKJ): *"Surely He shall deliver you from the snare of the fowler And from the perilous pestilence...No evil shall befall you. Nor shall any plague come near your dwelling: For He shall give His angels charge over you. To keep you in all your ways. They shall bear you up in their hands. Lest you dash your foot against a stone. You shall tread upon the lion and the cobra. The young lion and the serpent you shall trample under foot."*

To whom are these promises made?

They are directed to *"He who dwells in the secret place of the Most High"* (verse 1). They are also for those who set their love upon the Lord (verse 14). In other words, the promises are for those who actively love and abide in Him!

When you read a promise of God concerning your health or any other problem in your life, do not just read the promise. Read the entire chapter with its conditions which you must fulfill for God's power to be released!

Before you "claim" God's Word, search yourself to see if you have any "loose ends" or unfinished business with God in the areas of forgiveness or unrepented sin. Ask Him if there is something you can do for Him before you begin to appropriate His riches.

Follow a new guideline of love.

Whenever you want God to do something for you, ask yourself, "What can I do for God? What step of giving, faith, trust or obedience can I take right now so that His mighty resurrection power can be loosed in (and through) me?"

Then, as you search God's Word for further promises

which will meet your need, always keep two things foremost in your mind:

First, as someone who has been chosen and called into God's army, aim for the highest that His Word has to offer. Do not dwell or focus on the exceptions to His perfect will. Do not use the merciful exceptions to His perfect will as excuses for settling for anything less than His best for you.

Second, always seek to fulfill your part of the covenant relationship with as much vigor and enthusiasm as you seek His blessings. Remember that God's ultimate purpose is to draw you into loving, vital fellowship with Him, and good relationships are a two-way street of give and take.

God's perfect will for your finances

"But seek first the kingdom of God and His righteousness, and all these things shall be added to you" (Matthew 6:33, NKJ).

Of all the questions concerning God's perfect will for our lives, perhaps the one that causes the most misunderstanding is, "Doesn't God want me to be prosperous?"

We have already covered much of this topic in a previous chapter, but there are two additional points I would like to make.

The first point involves the crucial importance of asking what you can do to meet the conditions of God's promise, as we have just discussed. Failure to do so has resulted in indescribable heartache and frustration for so many people who have been deceived into thinking that all they have to do is "speak" God's Word and riches will be theirs.

For instance, one of the passages that people like to "claim" most often for their finances is the one from the book of Philippians which says, *"And my God shall supply all your need according to His riches in glory by Christ Jesus" (Philippians 4:19, NKJ).*

However, exactly what was it that inspired Paul to write this wonderful promise of God to these people? When we read the preceding verses we discover an amazing thing; namely, that these folks were some of the very few who stood behind Paul and totally backed him through previous sufferings.

In this letter, Paul commended them for sharing in his

distress, and told them, *"Now you Philippians know also that in the beginning of the gospel...no church shared with me concerning giving and receiving but you only...you sent aid once and again for my necessities"* (Philippians 4:15-16, NKJ).

After this commendation Paul bestowed the great blessing that all their needs would be met.

What we see vividly demonstrated in this chapter is God's basic, fundamental, unchangeable law of giving and receiving. Summed up in one sentence it says, *"Give, and it will be given to you..."* (Luke 6:38, NKJ).

Basically, this says that you reap what you sow. If you don't sow...you don't reap. Period. *"But this I say: He who sows sparingly will also reap sparingly, and he who sows bountifully will also reap bountifully"* (II Corinthians 9:6, NKJ).

From God's Word we also learn that receiving financial abundance is also linked to obedience in tithing (and to obedience in general). *" 'Bring all the tithes into the storehouse, That there may be food in My house, And prove me now in this,' Says the Lord of hosts, 'If I will not open for you the windows of heaven And pour out for you such blessing That there will not be room enough to receive it.' "* (Malachi 3:10, NKJ).

" 'And all these blessings shall come upon you and overtake you, because you obey the voice of the LORD your God...' " (Deuteronomy 28:2).

The second point about prosperity concerns motivation. That is, why do you want to be prosperous—for your own sake, or to please God with what you do with your prosperity?

The Apostle James warns us, *"You ask and do not receive, because you ask amiss, that you may spend it on your pleasures"* (James 4:3, NKJ).

God loves to supply His servants with an abundance. As the Psalmist sings, *"Let them shout for joy and be glad, Who favor my righteous cause; And let them say continually, 'Let the LORD be magnified, Who has pleasure in the prosperity of His servant' "* (Psalm 35:27, NKJ).

Believe me, God wants so much to prosper you. But He desires that you use your prosperity the way He uses His:

to be a blessing to the needy, and to build Christ's Kingdom to His glory!

Believe that *"...God is able to make all grace abound toward you, that you, always having all sufficiency in all things, have an abundance for every good work"* (II Corinthians 9:8, NKJ).

God's perfect will for your loved ones

"The Lord is not slack concerning His promise, as some count slackness, but is longsuffering toward us, not willing that any should perish but that all should come to repentance" (II Peter 3:9, NKJ).

Although we know from experience that not all people will accept salvation, it is still God's will to make every attempt to save them.

Keep in mind that our goal is to focus on (and to reach for) the highest that God has outlined in His Word. It is not our job to give up on anyone. Instead, we are to grow up into the unique challenge that each soul we meet presents to us.

Therefore, let us continue to "fight the good fight" for each unsaved loved one assigned to us by the Lord. For who are we to say how God is working behind the scenes of his or her heart?

He may be working through the witness of our own lives, even when we don't know it *(I Peter 3:1)*. Or perhaps He is sending laborers across his path, or using a tract found "accidentally" on the street.

We may never know the Lord's methods, but we do know that He desires all our loved ones to come into true knowledge of Him. We also know that, when we ask Him, He will give us many miraculous opportunities to be a vital link between these dying souls and eternal life.

God's perfect will for your marriage

"'For the LORD God of Israel says That He hates divorce, For it covers one's garment with violence,' Says the LORD of hosts. "Therefore take heed to your spirit, That you do not deal treacherously"' (Malachi 2:16, NKJ).

The entire subject of family harmony in today's society can be a most painful one for many of you. Yet again, we must always keep the image of God's highest will as our goal. According to His Word, His will is for families to stay together unified in love.

God does make some exceptions in cases of adultery. The Apostle Paul allowed separation in cases of desertion; but, in spite of these exceptions, God's perfect will never changes.

In this book we have talked a lot about the importance of being an overcomer. However, for some of you who are in deeply distressing situations (such as physical abuse and family violence), being an overcomer may seem like an impossible task.

If the forces of hell are coming against your family, don't give in! If necessary, seek competent biblical Christian counseling. Above all, don't try to fight alone.

Write to me so that my staff and I can pray with you. Know that we are standing with you through your roughest times. We long to join forces with you through your greatest battles. We are determined to see the works of the enemy completely defeated in your life.

Please, do not give up hope! Be courageous and take action...united action through the spirit of prayer. Be confident that through the power of the Holy Spirit, your family can become a great glory to God!

God's perfect will for your work—you are His endtime minister!

"As the Father has sent Me, I also send you" (John 20:21, NKJ).

Two thousand years ago, Christ's Church was vibrantly victorious through an army of lay ministers who were willing to reach out to the world in the full power of God's love. With that characteristic, they reached their entire known world in just 200 years.

Today we have 4.7 billion people on the face of this earth, and yet one-half of them have never heard the Name of Jesus! Something is wrong. Something is terribly wrong.

We must ask ourselves, "How could the early Church, without airplanes, without printing presses, without technology...even without Bibles...reach their whole world so quickly, while we sit in such a tragic state? What did they have that we don't have now?

What they had was a clear revelation from God of who a minister really is!

The Greek root of the word "minister" means "servant" or "to serve." The early Church knew that each one of them was ordained by God to serve...to minister...to manifest the living God to their fellow men.

Armed with this revelation, they didn't go out in their own power. They went out in the power of God's love. As a result, Satan's strongholds came crashing down throughout their world.

Do you think that God's perfect will for you as His endtime representative is any different than it was for them?

Do you think God gave them anything extra to fulfill His will that He hasn't given you?

I thank God for all the pastors and ordained ministers that we have today. But, if we are ever going to reach this world for God, we must be certain what His will is for each of us regarding Christian service. And we cannot do this until each one of us comes into a new revelation of who a minister really is!

Our understanding of a minister today is someone who goes through Bible school or a theological seminary, and is ordained by a denomination. After graduation he climbs into a pulpit and carries on business as usual.

Because of this, God's people have been lulled into thinking that it is God's will that they sit in the pews as sideline spectators. Week after week, month after month, they assume that this ordained theological student is the sole instrument that God wants to use to minister to the Body of Christ and to reach the world.

But are you ready for a bombshell? Are you willing to accept the fact that according to God's Word every person who confesses Jesus Christ to be his Lord and Savior, and who is filled with His Holy Spirit, is a minister and a priest of the living God?

You may find this shocking, but nowhere in the 93 uses of the word "minister" in the New Testament does it refer to the pastor of a church as we have coined it in our modern usage!

The truth is that it is God's will for **you** to be an ambassador for Christ, charged with the commission of doing your part to reconcile the lost sheep of this world to Him.

You are His endtime minister!

As a child of God, you now have the potential to be used

of our Lord in whatever job you do.

I love you so much that I want to see God's perfect plan for your life fulfilled. I want to see His Son's life grow in you, becoming mature and fruitful.

Are you a housewife, a doctor, a lawyer, a farmer, or a construction worker? Are you a businessman, a secretary, a bookkeeper, or a waitress? It doesn't matter what you do. God wants to do use you right where you are. The Bible says that *"His intention was the perfecting and the full equipping of the saints **(His consecrated people), (that they should do)** the work of ministering toward building up Christ's body **(the church)"** (Ephesians 4:12, TAB).*

Begin right now to be a minister of the Lord! Start by deciding that whatever you do, you will *"...do it heartily, as to the Lord and not to men, knowing that from the Lord you will receive the reward of the inheritance; for you serve the Lord Christ" (Colossians 3:23-24, NKJ).*

Believe God for His direction. Expect Him to use you in new ways every day with each person you meet! Our Lord's last instructions to His disciples were, *"...and you shall be witnesses to Me in Jerusalem, and in all Judea and Samaria, and to the end of the earth" (Acts 1:8, NKJ).* Ask yourself, "What are the areas of my spiritual Jerusalem'? Does it include my neighborhood? My workplace? The playground where my children go?"

"Who are the people in my 'territory'? Are they my in-laws? My children's friends? The clerks where I shop?"

Whoever they are, know that God has raised you up to bring and reflect His life to them. For you are one of His breakthrough people! You are a minister of our living Lord.

You were born to prove to the world through your life that Jehovah is **God**, and that Jesus Christ, His Son, lives. And this expression of Christ's powerful love in and through you is God's perfect will for your life.

Beloved, as we conclude our journey into discovering how you can know God's will for your life, let these words of the Holy Spirit be my fervent prayer for you:

"Now may the God of Peace who brought up our Lord Jesus from the dead, that great Shepherd of the Sheep, through the blood of the everlasting covenant, make you complete in every good work to do His will, working in you what is well pleasing in His sight, through Jesus Christ, to whom be glory forever and ever. Amen!" (Hebrews 13:20-21, NKJ).

...and God gave me a vision!

There is a greater anointing upon me now than ever before to pray for your needs.

Never before, in my more than 57 years of frontline ministry have I carried a deeper burden for the Body of Christ than I do now. I have prayed, fasted, interceded, agonized, and fought spiritual warfare against satanic powers...

...and God gave me a vision!

A vision of Jesus Christ, our Great High Priest, praying for all your needs.

God said, *"Place the needs of my people upon the altar before My Presence. Jesus is praying for all their needs to be met."*

Every need, every disease, every family problem, every circumstance... God wants me to lift your need for Jesus to pray for you. Do not delay. Write all your needs on the following page and mail it to me today!

For prayer call:
1-858-HELPLINE
1-858-435-7546

Brother Cerullo,

Please place these requests on the Miracle Prayer Altar in the World Prayer Center and pray for these needs:

_____

_____

_____

_____

_____

❏   I am standing with you. I agree we have to change the moral direction of America. We have to pray that God will SAVE AMERICA NOW!

❏   I will pray.

❏   Enclosed is an offering to help with the cost of the *SAVE AMERICA NOW!* campaign $/£_____.

Name _____

Address _____

City _____ State or Province _____

Postal Code _____ Phone Number (____)_____

E-mail_____

Fax _____

Mail today to:

MORRIS CERULLO WORLD EVANGELISM

San Diego: P.O. Box 85277 • San Diego, CA 92186

Canada: P.O. Box 3600 • Concord, Ontario L4K 1B6

U.K.: PO. Box 277 • Hemel Hempstead, Herts HP2 7DH

Web site: www.mcwe.com • **E-mail:** morriscerullo@mcwe.com

For prayer call: **1-858-HELPLINE HELPLINE FAX: 1-858-427-0555**
435-7546

HELPLINE EMAIL: helpline@mcwe.com

Tear off and and mail this in today!

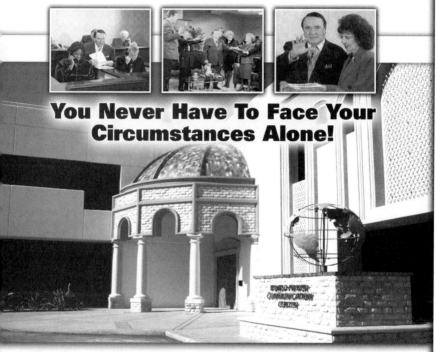